Principals under Pressure

The Growing Crisis

Alexander W. Wiseman

ScarecrowEducation
Lanham, Maryland • Toronto • Oxford
2005

Published in the United States of America
by ScarecrowEducation
An imprint of The Rowman & Littlefield Publishing Group, Inc.
4501 Forbes Boulevard, Suite 200, Lanham, Maryland 20706
www.scarecroweducation.com

PO Box 317
Oxford
OX2 9RU, UK

British Library Cataloguing in Publication Information Available

Library of Congress Cataloging-in-Publication Data

Wiseman, Alexander W., 1968–
  Principals under pressure : the growing crisis / Alexander W. Wiseman.
    p. cm.
  Includes bibliographical references and index.
  ISBN 1-57886-183-7 (pbk. : alk. paper)
  1. School principals—United States. 2. School management and
organization—United States. 3. Educational leadership—United States.
I. Title.
  LB2831.62.W58 2005
  371.2'012—dc22   2004014213

for becky

Contents

Preface
Reflecting on School Principals

American principals are in peril. They are in peril of becoming victims of the growing accountability policies in the United States. They are in peril of believing the hype about their own importance and power. They are in peril of becoming heavy-handed demagogues in largely democratic educational systems. This is the growing crisis for school principals in America. There is, however, an alternative—but it requires that educational policymakers, researchers, and the concerned public ask themselves what kind of school principals they want their children to have. Do they want schools to be run by principals focused strictly on high achievement and firm discipline? Is it okay for principals to lose perspective on the type of students and community their schools serve?

While most would agree that performance and discipline are important elements of every school, few want a principal who focuses only on one agenda to the exclusion of other important issues such as safety, faculty development, or even athletic and extracurricular opportunities for students. Yet the images of "good" principals reinforced in movies, television, books, and even much of the professional literature are larger-than-life, idealistic stereotypes.

While books and articles touting the benefits of strong "leadership" have dominated popular principal literature, the managerial activity of principals is a topic of increasing importance but little attention. One of the reasons that management rather than leadership has become more important is that the activities and behaviors traditionally ascribed to principals are increasingly shared by other members of the school.

As more and more policymakers, researchers, and educators realize that the managerial functions in schools are being spread among the traditionally nonmanagerial professionals (like the eternal fall guys: teachers), it is increasingly important to know what exactly it is that school principals must do as managers, why they do it, what the models for school principals' managerial behavior are, and what the boundaries for this managerial behavior are.

The current state of knowledge about school principals is largely anecdotal and frequently consists of individual case studies, observations, or interviews. In particular, there have been few empirical or quantitative studies done in an internationally comparative context. Some researchers have tried to analyze principals in specific nations, but an international as well as a comparative perspective of American school principals is missing. In an era when educators at all levels have the information and ability to borrow from other schools', districts', and nations' education systems, it is surprising that there are not many examinations of American principals in light of international trends.

This book presents the arguments, rationales, and explanations for what American principals do by looking at the international context in which the American educational system is situated and in which American school principals operate. It presents a combination of background, theoretical perspective, data analysis, and policy recommendations founded on evidence derived from empirical research.

This book is written in the hope that policymakers and principals will use the information provided here to (1) decide which managerial activities are the most effective uses of school principals' time and efforts, (2) decide which managerial activities are the most appropriate given the unique context of the schools and systems in which principals operate, and (3) benchmark the activity of school principals by region or district against the average levels of managerial activity and its effectiveness in each nation and the international community as a whole.

Students, researchers, and scholars can use the information provided in this book to (1) understand the relationship between organizational environment and what school principals do, (2) develop new analyses and theories related to the managerial activity and behavior of school principals, and (3) develop and recommend policy reform related to school principals' management activities. It is my intention to provide a contextual framework that will allow researchers and academics to understand what American principals, in particular, do by understanding the blend of global, national, and local conditions that uniquely tailor the needs of school communities and students and the pressures to which principals typically respond.

This book is not a treatise on the dos and don'ts of leadership. It is an attempt to situate principals' behavior within the contexts of global competition and trends that characterize schools around the world, including those in the United States. Those looking for the "seven traits of highly effective leaders" or "ten ways principals can raise reading achievement" will be disappointed. This book presents a critical but supportive perspective on the state and future of school principals. It will give readers a fresh look at school principals, especially in the context of the pressures and trends that cross school district and system boundaries.

Readers will notice a downplaying of the more popular and possibly damaging influence that books on school "leadership" often have on principals and their preparation. This means that the contents of this book are sometimes critical of some of the other professional literature on principals, especially in America. I do not use the terms *charisma* or *leader* lightly. There is a bias in the literature that this book tries to avoid as a whole. This bias says that principals must be charismatic, visionary leaders in order to accomplish anything valid or good. This, in my opinion and according to research, is wrong.

Charismatic, visionary leaders are not commonplace, and, without detracting from the accomplishments of those principals who are these sorts of leaders, the fact of the matter is that some of the best principals in the world are excellent managers. Being a principal is not about taking personal charge as much as it is about assembling and directing an excellent team and providing trusted team members with the resources and opportunities to do the best work they are capable of doing. The ability to be invisible, or to "lead from behind," is one of the best characteristics that many "good" principals have. This book explains why this is so and provides principles to avert the growing crisis for American school principals.

Acknowledgments

There are many people who deserve thanks for their help and support throughout the process of writing this book. It has not been a smooth ride either. There are many vested interests that raise high the banner of educational "leadership." Those interests are not always supportive of alternative perspectives on school principals, leadership, or administration. But American school principals deserve to be told the truth. They deserve to be supported both professionally and personally. And now there are a number of growing voices that do just that without catering to special interest groups. This book is among those voices in support of American school principals.

The most loving and supportive stakeholder in this project has been and continues to be my wife, Becky. Due to her inspiration I have embarked on most of the adventures (both academic and otherwise) that I have in life. Her love and support have brought me through more than can be imagined—much more than is represented by this book. Becky continues to be the guiding light in front of me and the driving force lifting me toward the finish line for every project I take on. She deserves every ounce of credit for this book (and none of the blame).

My mother, Cindy, has also been a strong support and is responsible for inspiring me to value education and educators from an early age. Her intelligent approach to life has set the bar high throughout my life, and she continues to provide constructive criticism and new ideas even today.

This work would not be possible without my mentors, colleagues, and friends who have been faithful and friendly critics of my work for

many years. I thank Gerald K. LeTendre for showing me how to perse-
vere and defend my ideas even in the face of criticism. I thank Naif H.
Alromi for grounding me in real-world policy and constantly questioning my ideas and approaches to school principals and leadership.

In particular, I would like to thank David P. Baker. David took me on
as a green graduate student and patiently showed me how he thinks
about education and research—the most valuable learning experience
of my career. I am thankful for his example and support in the development of my own ideas and perspectives. He also instilled in me an
appreciation for institutional theory for which I am continually grate-
ful, and continues to be my most valuable critic.

I thank my School of Education colleagues at the University of
Tulsa: Diane Beals, David Brown, Warren Hipsher, and Shirley Ro-
bards. They have been both my mentors and my colleagues, which has
made their support and advice that much more valuable. Some have
taken the time to carefully read and critique draft manuscripts of this
book, and some have served as inspirations simply through their own
examples of professionalism and scholarship.

I would also like to thank Fred Droege for the many hours of discussion and review that he freely gave. In particular, the final chapter
would not have been possible without his suggestions and insight.

And finally, I would like to thank the University of Tulsa's Henry
Kendall College of Arts & Sciences and the Office of Research and
Sponsored Programs for graciously supporting this project through two
Summer Faculty Development Fellowships.

Any errors in the work presented here are, of course, exclusively
mine.

THE AMERICAN SCHOOL PRINCIPAL CRISIS

Principals must handle discipline, [individual education plans], enrollment, ordering and purchasing, hiring and evaluating teachers,
building maintenance, the needs of parents. . . . Then we're also
supposed to be instructional leaders totally familiar with and expert
in leading discussions about curriculum and teaching practices.

—Lolli Haws, principal

What history tells us is that the traditional hierarchical model of
school leadership, in which identified leaders in positions of formal
authority make critical improvement decisions and then seek,
through various strategies, to promote adherence to those decisions
among those who occupy the rungs on the ladder below, has failed
to adequately answer the repeated calls for sweeping educational
improvements across American schools. While one can locate out-
posts of excellence where maverick principals or superintendents
have resurrected dying schools or districts through these types of
strategies, such efforts are recognizable only because they are the
exception not the rule.

—Michael A. Copland

What are school principals doing? And how do we know if they are doing
it well or not? Consider the recommendations of policymakers regarding
the role of principals in the ongoing reform in American public schools.
These popular recommendations have increasingly called for accountability for school leaders, especially principals—but accountability for

what? It is hard to hold someone accountable for work that cannot be consistently defined or objectively measured.

The United States is not alone in singling out principals for special responsibility. In particular, pay-for-performance schemes have attracted attention around the world, but in the United States a growing number of states and districts are focusing more and more on the accountability of principals and tying principals' jobs to students' performance gains.

What many of these calls for accountability overlook is that how school principals really do their job depends on the schools' context. School context is made up of the type of students, the community resources, the quality of the staff, and many other characteristics unique to each school. Because school contexts vary so much, and in the United States locally determined funding further exacerbates differences between schools, the way many principals manage their schools is more like selecting from a menu than setting a strategic course. Like a restaurant menu, there are several different and conflicting choices that American school principals can make. There are still categories of behavior and management activity that principals usually choose from, just as there are types of food on a menu that diners usually order. If there are categories to choose from and choices are determined by school contexts, then what do school principals really do? In spite of the democratic and localized character of the American school system, it appears that school principals' hands are forced by school context or tied by school policies.

In spite of this paradox, many have arisen to tell principals what they should do. Countless books and articles provide laundry lists of behaviors that so-called "effective" or "successful" principals should employ. School leadership has become an industry in and of itself. But the menu approach to school management is a dangerous one. In short, there is a growing crisis for American school principals because they are increasingly and individually being held accountable for activities, behaviors, and performance over which they have little individual control.

Criticizing the popular perspective of principal as a "change agent" and "leader" is a rare exercise, but it is important for getting a proper perspective on school principals and what they do. While these criticisms are valid and should be discussed more prominently than they often are, it is still important to know and be familiar with the literature that perpetuates these myths. Why? Because research and writing dedicated to these sorts of visionary statements and leadership concepts continue to dominate the thinking about school principals. And because these are the dominant writings on school principals, they are influential in creating the system of school management and influencing individual principals in schools across the United States and around the world.

Consider groundbreaking thinker Thomas Sergiovanni's classic book, *Leadership for the Schoolhouse*, an interesting addition to the canon of popular "school leadership" scholarship. In it, Sergiovanni asserts that leading a school should have to do with knowing the students and community rather than maintaining power and status at the top of the organizational hierarchy. At the time of its publication, this was a welcome breath of fresh air to many principals, policymakers, and educational researchers who saw the need to contextualize principal behavior rather than rely on school principals' assertiveness and individual charisma to push through school reforms and take schools forward into the new millennium. The new millennium has arrived, but much of the public, policymakers, and even many principals themselves have lost Sergiovanni's initial message. Many no longer have the ability or motivation to think about school principals outside of categories listed in the "menu" of principal types advocated by schools of education, school boards and superintendents, parents, business, and the popular media.

Like Sergiovanni's work, this book provides an opportunity for educational policymakers, researchers, the general public, and school principals themselves to *think* about principals in a new way. Unlike Sergiovanni's work, this book shows what the conventional wisdom about school principals is and how it contributes to the growing crisis for American school principals.

Part 1 explains how American school principals are becoming increasingly heavy-handed, and how a shift from emphasizing leadership to emphasizing management might save American principals and their schools with them. It is ironic that in the most democratic and localized educational system in the world the growing problem is autocratic control over schools. This is the direction in which many

American school principals are headed. The pressure to perform is strong in the United States, and getting stronger with every new educational accountability plan springing up in district after district across America, and appears even more intense when compared to other nations around the world.

CHAPTER 1

Getting a Perspective on Principals

Who can recognize the truth about American schools? Anyone who can is an exception to the rule. Most Americans cannot. In fact, it is decidedly unpopular in America to tell the truth about schools. Annual polls of Americans show that the nation's schools are generally seen as average or worse. Respected newspapers report that in international studies of academic achievement, American students rank in the middle or lower in international rankings. Popular late-night talk shows garner huge ratings for segments in which "average" American students are asked basic questions and fail. Yet none of these examples represents the truth about American schools.

Schooling in America is not only a right; it is a requirement. As a result, almost everybody in America has spent at least twelve years of his or her life in school. All people have war stories, most embarrassing moments, greatest triumphs, and most infamous escapades from their days in school. Important lessons about everything from algebra to dating all took place in school. Every person who is a product of the American school system believes that the time and effort spent there qualifies him or her to pass judgment on the quality of schooling in America. In spite of these extensive and meaningful experiences in schools, the public still largely misunderstands how schools work and what they do. This is not surprising. How many people who shop at Wal-Mart understand shipping, marketing, or accounting? As a nation, Americans are widespread consumers of education. Few are experts in the administration, methods, or evaluation of education.

Now consider the truth about American schools. The truth is that American students outperform their international counterparts in most areas. The truth is that American schools improve with every passing decade. The truth is that American principals are some of the most competent and well-educated principals in the world. But as research and writing on principals has developed, it has become popular to either reach out to the struggling school administrator or capitalize on the lay public's morbid fascination with so-called "failing" American schools.

To solve these alleged problems in American education, principals are called on to lead their schools out of a perceived educational morass. Most of what has been said and written about school principals in the United States is tainted by an expectation that they should be charismatic, visionary leaders capable of accomplishing the impossible. Various terms, formulas, articles, and books have appeared that elaborate on school principal "leadership." Prescriptions and recommendations for how to "lead" schools are widespread, but rarely does this conventional wisdom focus on what American school principals really do and how they impact student learning.

Instead there is a growing tendency on the part of the public and policymakers to hold school principals accountable for the performance of teachers and students in their schools. Principals in some school districts in America are even held accountable for gains in achievement test scores of students. In spite of the popular idea that principals can lead their schools to newfound success against all of the odds, there is little evidence of this beyond exceptional and anecdotal accounts. In fact, there is relatively little data-driven research showing that school principals are the influential instructional leaders they have been made out to be. Missing evidence, however, has not stopped principals from being held accountable for the performance of teachers and students in their schools.

THE HEAVY-HANDED SYNDROME

In response to ever-increasing pressure for schools to "improve," principals are wielding tighter and tighter control over what goes on in their schools. In the most extreme cases, they become benevolent dictators of their tiny kingdoms, wielding a heavy hand to meet accountability standards. This sort of heavy-handed "leadership" is the greatest crisis for American school principals, and it is like a cancer spreading throughout the educational system.

Heavy-handed principals often micromanage their schools. They want to approve all the lessons that are taught. They want to be consulted on every disciplinary action taken. They want to take away the autonomy that teachers and others who work in schools have come to love about their jobs. If they cannot effect change (e.g., gains in student achievement scores) in any of these ways, they become desperate. They begin trying to deceive the parents, the district administrators, and anyone else to whom they are accountable.

An example of how accountability expectations lead to heavy-handed leadership among school principals was reported in the *New York Times* (Winerip, 2003). In Houston, Texas, the heart of George W. Bush's educational initiative, No Child Left Behind, in the very district where the U.S. Secretary of Education was once superintendent, a huge scandal broke out.

The Texas Department of Education established a policy that schools with high dropout rates would be audited because the taxpayers of Texas deserve to get what they pay for. The local school district in Houston established policies that put principals on one-year, performance-based contracts. In addition, the school district raised the expectations for schools and principals through yearly mandates on such things as student attendance and dropout rates. The immediate school context made meeting these mandated standards difficult, if not impossible. The schools in this district typically served low-income, highly mobile immigrant communities where dropouts are common. The influence of the overall school environment shaped what these principals did. When offered a lose-lose dilemma, school principals in this Houston district found that the only win option was to lie. School principals were falsifying school records in an attempt to reduce the reported dropout rates for their schools. This type of principal activity was happening in more than one school in this district.

Conventional wisdom idealizes American school principals as benevolent autocrats, justly ruling their educational kingdoms. The problem is that autocrats (benevolent or not) rarely thrive in democratic systems, and school systems in the United States and around the world are largely founded on democratic principles. From a more critical point of view, school principals have been called "pharaohs obsessed with preserving pyramids of power" (Buchen, 2000). Strangely enough, it is the local autonomy in the American educational system that puts American school principals, in particular, in danger of being drawn into the heavy-handed syndrome. The more that new federal and state educational policies push responsibility for schooling to the local school district and to individual schools, the more that principals are held accountable for school and student performance, and the more that principals become heavy-handed leaders.

THE COMPLEXITY OF SCHOOL ENVIRONMENTS

Previous thinking has not fully considered the influence that the complexity of school environments has on what school principals do. By *school environment* is meant the social, political, and economic context in which principals and schools operate. It is important to understand, as figure 1 shows, that school environments are multilevel, meaning that there are many layers to a school's environment. These layers can be defined according to the characteristics of each level. The first level is the school itself and the social, political, and economic norms that are unique to that school. For example, in some schools there is an at-

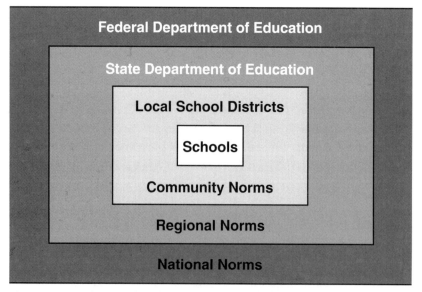

Figure 1.   *The Multilevel Organizational Nesting of Schools.*

mosphere of healthy competitive achievement among the students and teachers, while in others the attitude is more about just getting by.

The next level of a school's environment is the local community. In most American examples this includes the whole school district. Each school's community will have its own social, political, and economic norms that surround and permeate everything that happens at the local school. When this happens, the school's own norms are "nested" within the school district's norms. The school environment is a multilevel context of nested relationships. Key to understanding the nested aspect of school environments is understanding that what happens at each level of the school system happens within the context of and is nested within each successive layer.

The pattern of multiple environmental levels and nested relationships at each level of schooling adds to the complexity of a school's environment. In schools characterized by healthy competition, the local community atmosphere may be permeated by an appreciation for the value of education or the importance of a college education. This atmosphere will usually reflect the collective attitude of parents as well as business community leaders. The nested nature of school environments means that the school-level atmosphere of healthy competitive achievement both exists and takes shape because of the school-level environment and vice versa. The influence of nested environments is not one-way.

School environments are often without clear borders. For example, how can the degree of influence that parents, neighbors, and state-level policymakers have on schools be compared to the degree of influence that principals have? Although some research does estimate relationships between what school principals do and the individual elements of schools' immediate environments, researchers have yet to determine how principals adjust their activities in complex school environments comprising many different levels and even conflicting norms at each level.

The lack of clarity regarding school environments allows schools and policymakers to debate what principals should be doing without necessarily creating a "right" or a "wrong" idea about them. In other words, there is no blueprint for school principals—or at least there should not be. Each school presents unique challenges within a succession of unique and nested environments. What may work perfectly for the urban principal may get the suburban principal fired, and vice versa. Or what may work for the urban principal in one city may not work for an urban principal in another city, and so on.

The one common element across schools' unique environments is that the public believes that schooling in America is failing overall but doing relatively well in their own communities (Rose & Gallup, 2003). This conflict in public perception and expectation is enhanced by the conflict between social, political, and economic norms at each level of a school's environment. In this sort of shaky situation, what is a principal supposed to do other than clamp down on teachers and students? Knowing what school principals actually do and how American school principals are unique can help answer these sorts of questions.

AMERICAN PRINCIPALS IN COMPARATIVE CONTEXT

Principals are the highest ranking administrative officials at individual schools. Many principals in the United States are former teachers and most are male. Few have specific training in management, but that number is rising. In many schools there is more than one principal. When there is more than one principal, there are two main options. The first is to have the principals share responsibility and status. These are called co-principals. A second option is to organize principals hierarchically, typically with one principal and one or more vice-principals. Although the reason for having a vice-principal is often to distinguish between those providing "direction" (the principal) and those enforcing policy (the vice-principal), to avoid confusion the term "school principal" can be used to mean any or all of the principals at a given school.

Principals in other nations may not be as administratively bent as American school principals; they may be more like "head teachers" or they may play more of a symbolic role in a larger bureaucratic system. The dominant characteristic shared by American principals that sets them apart from principals in other nations is the extreme amount of decision-making autonomy that they have, at least officially. This autonomy is a consequence of the drastic localization inherent in the American educational system. A related characteristic of American school principals that makes them unique is the extreme responsibility and accountability that they have for the performance of their schools and students. This is largely a product of their extreme decision-making autonomy, which principals in other nations do not have.

To begin thinking about how school principals in the United States are uniquely American, consider for a moment an example of the differences between American and Japanese school principals and what makes these differences important. First, ask why comparing American school principals with principals in another country like Japan might be of interest. One reason that has been offered in the past that specifically applies to an American–Japanese comparison is that Japan is a consistent high achiever on international assessments of math and science. Japanese students score at the top of every international assessment they participate in.

Another reason to be interested in a comparison with Japan is the economic competition between the United States and Japan. Many East Asian nations were compared with the United States by researchers in the late 1980s and early 1990s because these "Asian tigers" had some of the fastest growing economies in the world. This economic prosperity coincided with reports of their students' high achievement levels in math and science in particular. Studies comparing the educational systems in Japan and the United States became common in educational research. In fact, American teachers and school principals started traveling to Japan themselves to visit and learn from Japanese schools.

A second question to ask when comparing school principals between nations might be about the unique characteristics of each nation's educational system. For instance, the Japanese educational system has two predominant characteristics: centralized decision-making and high stakes testing. Two related but contrasting characteristics describe schooling in the United States: localized decision-making and low stakes advancement. Sometimes social promotion is even a problem in American schools, meaning that teachers and others will promote students from one grade to the next in order to keep the student with an age-appropriate cohort regardless of the students' academic qualification or readiness.

Another important question to ask is how do the social, political, and economic contexts or environments of the schools in each nation compare. In Japan, for example, there is a cultural expectation that students will work extremely hard to achieve high grades and that their families will not only support their studies, but will also push the students to excel beyond what they might otherwise do. In the United States, students, parents, and teachers believe in the importance of individual achievement and independence in terms of motivation and persistence in schooling. There is often little family support, or the family support that American students get is characteristic of their socioeconomic status more than a general cultural norm emphasizing schooling and academic achievement. The influence of these complex school environments on school principals' activities is important at both the local and national levels.

WHAT IS RIGHT WITH AMERICAN SCHOOL PRINCIPALS?

It is important in any discussion of American schooling to truthfully acknowledge how well American students do and how well American teachers teach given the extreme variation in school resources, student backgrounds, and teacher interests in the United States. This all occurs under the vigilant and responsible care of school principals across America. It is also amazing how well school principals are able to make the best of whatever they get from their school district support— financial or otherwise. There is often not a lot of extra support coming from district, state, or national levels for school principals, but they hold the ship together, so to speak, and keep the schools running as smoothly as possible in spite of the distractions.

It would be a crime not to mention how much of an American school principal's time is spent "putting out fires" and appeasing parents and others who have a stake in the education of America's youth. When policymakers and the public utter the word "accountability" regarding education, among the first targets are school principals. In some states and districts, principals' jobs depend on how well others perform (e.g., student test scores). Assuming that what principals do causes students to perform well is a touchy issue. This is like saying that parents should be required to go to jail if their children commit crimes, or that a hotel manager should be fired for the bad behavior (or rewarded for the good behavior) of the hotel guests. While there may be a link between the actions of one person and the performance of another, there is little evidence that directly links school principals' activity with individual students' performance.

American school principals are doing the right thing when they strive to improve student achievement, but they are doing even better things by keeping the public in touch with the schools. Some say they should be rewarded for creating learning environments that teachers and students can work in. School principals are rarely given the credit they deserve for staying after school late to attend most if not all of the schools' extracurricular activities. School principals sacrifice, and sacrifice, and sacrifice. This may be one of the reasons why there is a principal shortage in many districts across America.

Unfortunately, there are some not-so-shining moments in the lives of American school principals, too. Critics of school principals say maybe they should not be praised so highly for simply doing their job, which is what is expected of them. Maybe what is wrong with American school principals is that they are expected to do too much and as a result spread themselves too thin. Can a principal be the glue that holds a crumbling school together while also being a labor negotiator among the faculty and staff or a public relations expert with the district school board, parents, and every community citizen who has an opinion about education?

American school principals often have a hard time delegating responsibility. They do not share the responsibility for their schools very easily, and as a result many of the characteristics that look so good when we discuss what is right with American school principals also look terribly wrong when lumped all together. Who thinks that a restaurant owner can survive if she is the cook, the wait staff, the cleaning crew, the advertising manager, and all of the other employees that are needed to run a restaurant all rolled into one? There is no way this can be done, and in fact it should not even be attempted. The restaurant owner would collapse from exhaustion and the restaurant itself would probably go out of business.

For one person to assume responsibility for all of the functions of an organization is ludicrous. Yet this is what American school principals increasingly do. Part of the reason they do this is that they are expected to, but part of it is that this is how they have been shown or trained to be school principals. Perhaps they do not know any better. If so, then they are ignorant. Perhaps they really think they can do it all alone. If so, then they are arrogant. Perhaps they do not know how else to do the best they can for their school. If so, then they are shortsighted.

What is wrong with American school principals is that they are not expected to simply be managers of what is already a very complex organization. They and the public they serve have a vision of effective, charismatic leadership. But this vision is deceptive, and it leads to unnecessary pressure on school principals. Unfortunately, a result of this pressure on principals to hold the reigns of their schools is that they hold on too tightly. They become heavy-handed leaders who hurt either their schools, their teachers, their students, themselves, or all of the above.

Why do heavy-handed principals ultimately fail? The answer has more to do with the fundamental organization and ideology of schooling than with the individual principals. Most educational systems are set up to be relatively democratic and to be locally controlled, although many people, even at high levels of the American system, do not understand that. This is why there are state and local school boards and administrative districts in the United States, and regional administrative boards and units in many other nations as well, rather than just one centralized administrative unit with all of the decision-making authority for a nation of schools. Even in relatively centralized systems, such as those in Japan or France, there are still local or regional administrative units that decide how to implement policy from above.

As the contemporary version of modern mass schooling has spread around the world, one of the most impressive elements of democracy in each nation has been the input of the public into its school systems. This public permeability at the local school level has served as a defense against using schools solely to indoctrinate youth with the dominant culture's social, political, or economic agendas. In addition, localizing governance has given principals more authority to customize schooling as necessary, but also more control over their schools and the administration and instruction that goes on at their schools.

A gradual process whereby power (educational and otherwise) is centralized and authority is localized occurs throughout the history of education in the United States as well as in other national educational systems that have adopted the modern mass schooling model. This convergence of state policy occurs simultaneously with a divergence of authority for policy implementation, and it is accompanied by increasing levels of stratification of authority for each level of separation between state power and local school authority. This process begins, necessarily, with the imposition and exercise of power.

So what is the difference between what is right and what is wrong with American school principals? The answer is: very little. This is the part that scares those who think critically about American school principals. School principals who are vigilant and responsible, who make do with less than they need in terms of resources and support, and who go the extra mile when they have already run a marathon are the school principals who get burned out, who end up making lousy decisions through bloodshot eyes, and who desperately micromanage every aspect of administration, teaching, and learning in their schools. It is a little like the answer to the standard job interview question that asks aspiring employees to describe their greatest weaknesses. Everyone who anticipates this question answers that their biggest fault is taking their strengths too far. In the case of the American school principal, this is true. What is right and what is wrong with American school principals are two sides of the same coin, which is dangerous for the principals as well as for the future of American education.

The American school principal crisis is a result of many contributing factors, even though the conflict in expectations and pressures on school principals is the visible result of it all. The biggest contribution to this crisis comes from the forced blending of achievement, accountability, and access expectations. School principals are expected to increase student achievement and school performance, and they are held accountable for this increase, while simultaneously being subjected to the whims and fancies of the general public via unprecedented access to even the most mundane activities that school principals perform.

Part of the road to recovery for principals is to better understand what principals do, how and why they do it, and what the contexts for principal behavior are. Understanding is important, because with objective information on school principals, policymakers and the public can make more informed decisions about what they expect principals to do, principals can consciously think about what they do and how they do it, and school administration can begin to be revised as a real profession with reasonable goals, structure, and support rather than a formulaic recipe vaguely calling for a teaspoon of "leadership" mixed with a cup of "charisma." The first step toward understanding what principals do and how they are being carried in the direction they are is to understand what is expected of school principals in America, in particular.

CHAPTER 2

Expectations for American School Principals

American school principals are uniquely American. This may seem obvious, but what makes them so different from principals in other parts of the world? These differences are important because they are the reasons that there is an *American* school principal crisis. Knowing what makes American principals unique can also help identify the solutions to this crisis.

As symbolic figureheads as well as high-ranking administrative officials, American principals have a defining characteristic: they are expected to do too much. These expectations come from every part of schools and society. Parents expect principals to tailor the school to their children's academic, physical, social, and emotional needs. Teachers expect principals to provide them with support, resources, and opportunities. Local community leaders expect principals to provide schooling that prepares students to lead productive lives after school, both in the workplace and in higher education. Superintendents and school board members expect principals to implement educational policy and monitor compliance with this policy. And the list goes on.

My first meaningful encounter with this expectation phenomenon came through a personal experience as a first-year high school teacher in a rural school district. My principal, whom I will call Mr. Bowman although that is not his real name, was also new to our school and had previously been a respected principal at another school. Mr. Bowman believed the popular assumptions about and expectations for American school principals. He had a strong vision for the future of our school, and he believed that he could lead our school to higher achievement scores, better classroom teaching, and district-wide dominance. We had faculty meetings and one-day retreats focusing on concepts like "synergy" and "success." And although Mr. Bowman was fired-up about school improvement and student achievement, the school board fired him before Christmas of his first year.

Mr. Bowman's "leadership" style was just one of the many factors that contributed to his swift departure, but in hindsight it was a significant one. In his zeal to reform our school, Mr. Bowman acted like the "ideal" American principal according to popular expectations and assumptions. His style, based on his own comments, was founded on a corporate leadership model, which unfortunately meant that he became "heavy-handed."

By all accounts, Mr. Bowman was the poster child for leadership and efficiency as a school principal. For example, Mr. Bowman was very mobile. He walked the halls, visited classrooms, checked the campus, and was generally never in his office. This sounds like a very proactive style, but it became a significant part of his undoing with the faculty. Any teacher who wanted to meet with Mr. Bowman had to "walk and talk," and this as much as any other thing ignited the teachers' lounge. Some actual teachers' comments were:

"If he really wanted to listen to us, he'd sit down with us."

"I can't get a word in edgewise with him stopping in every classroom we pass."

"He walks so fast, I can't keep up."

Then there was the little issue of the four-inch knife. I happened to be the teacher on duty that morning who discovered the student with the knife on school grounds. This same student had made threatening comments to a teacher just the previous week. Our school had a zero-tolerance policy, but Mr. Bowman thought this student deserved another chance. Instead of following school policy and expelling the student, he only suspended the student for a few days. Mr. Bowman's "vision" put his personal policies above school policy. The teachers went crazy. They complained and asked how Mr. Bowman could let this student stay when he had already threatened a teacher and now had been caught with a weapon on campus.

Unfortunately for Mr. Bowman, he believed that he was individually responsible for the school and that as the accountable "leader" of the school he could make independent decisions regardless of school or district policies. After all, he believed he was being a strong, visionary leader. Mr. Bowman had read much of the effective schools and instructional leadership literature. He was on the cutting edge of the latest business leadership techniques. But in the end, he was a terrible school principal. What Mr. Bowman did not know was how to manage a school within the context of that individual school's community and culture.

SCHOOL PRINCIPALS IN AN ACCOUNTABILITY CULTURE

American school principals like Mr. Bowman live and work within an educational system founded on unique beliefs. American idealism emphasizes the romanticized but often unrealistic idea that we are a nation of individuals. This emphasis on the importance of individuals, which is called "individual exceptionalism," leads to an assumption that responsibility for an organization may be individualized as well.

Another unique American belief is a result of the dominant economic perspective in the United States: market-driven capitalism. When individual exceptionalism blends with market-driven capitalist ideology, individual accountability for performance becomes a part of the conventional wisdom. For example, a prevailing belief among educational administrators and policymakers is that schools can or should be run like corporations. A second and related belief is that school principals are like corporate CEOs, where "the buck stops." Not everyone who holds this belief will state it as boldly as this, but assumptions that draw on Americans' deep roots in market-driven ideology and individual exceptionalism inevitably lead to discussions about accountability.

The ideologies behind schooling in the United States complement the core American notions of individual exceptionalism and market-driven accountability. Most important is the fact that the American education system has been purposefully created to allow and encourage public penetration of this mass, compulsory institution. From this blending of ideology with schooling comes a culture of accountability for students and teachers, but especially for school principals. The characteristic American expectation that principals are like school CEOs, coupled with the mass, compulsory, and publicly permeable character of the American school system, leads to a lot of accountability talk regarding American school principals.

School principals are held accountable for student performance, school safety, teacher effectiveness, curriculum content, and a school's reputation in the community, to name a few. In particular, the ongoing standards and accountability movement in the United States, with its emphasis on performance at the individual, classroom, and school levels, suggests that academic achievement scores are the most important measure of school principals' performance.

Among many professional educators and community members alike, the relationship between what principals do and how students perform has become a given rather than an assumption. Although existing research suggests that there is no consistent relationship between what principals do and how well students perform, scholars have introduced the concept of schools having an organizational environment. School administration professionals, policymakers, and the American public rarely get this message. Instead, conventional wisdom follows on the misleading assumption that principals should be visionary leaders who are responsible for leading their schools, in spite of overwhelming odds, toward continual gains in student achievement scores and high placement in district, state, and national rankings. Few stop to consider why school principals do what they do and how expecting more from them than they are actually capable of could work counter to even the best principal's intentions and be harmful to schools, teachers, students, and the principals themselves.

There are three expectations for American school principals that combine to form this American culture of accountability. These expectations result from the uniquely American beliefs outlined above and build on one another. The first is the achievement expectation. The second is the access expectation. And the third is the accountability expectation. These three expectations constitute a tall order for school principals.

THE ACHIEVEMENT EXPECTATION

As schooling becomes and remains the dominant formal mechanism by which citizens are formed, socialized, and prepared for adult life, the governance of schools becomes increasingly important. The resulting pressure on principals to influence and, it is hoped, improve the instruction of students is significant. This notion of principals as instructional leaders has become the conventional perspective of principals, although the terms used to describe it change every few years. The conventional approach suggests that how principals govern schools affects the resources and opportunities available to students, which then influence student learning measured as student achievement.

The conventional perspective of school principals in the American culture of accountability suggests that as a result of what school principals do, students should perform well, their achievement scores should improve in relation to established performance benchmarks, and these achievement gains should continue year after year. But the twenty-million-dollar question is whether or not principals can do what needs to be done to improve student performance and whether or not they should be held accountable for this kind of sustained performance. If indeed principals are expected to influence the achievement of students, then they must also be expected to shape the instruction that is offered by teachers. If principals are expected to influence student achievement, then they must have some sort of effect on the cumulative learning of students throughout their educational careers. And if principals are expected to influence student achievement, then there must be a justifiable record of this sort of relationship between principals and student achievement suggesting that it is possible in the first place.

To determine if principals are indeed accountable for the instruction, learning, and achievement of students in their schools requires more than simple opinion or wishful thinking about what principals should or ought to do. It requires that there be carefully analyzed evidence showing that principals do effect change in student performance and that this change is specifically positive.

There are those who argue quite vehemently that principals do make a difference in student performance. The assumption on the part of some of these proponents of a causal link between principals and performance is that if principals do not make a difference, then they are worthless or in danger of losing status, respect, or worse. Proponents of this causal link use this argument to validate the purpose of principals. It is a rather straightforward argument that makes critics sometimes wonder if causal link proponents are worried that principals will be done away with if a link is not made. In some nations, this is perhaps a real threat. In the United States and other traditional systems of universal, compulsory education, it is hardly possible that the principal's place in the school administration would so easily be done away with.

If principals do not have any direct impact on student performance—or if they have only an indirect impact—the role and responsibility of school principals will not culminate in student achievement. But because this conventional achievement expectation is strong in educational administration, related policy, and research, accountability expectations for school principals are not far behind. Regardless of the cause, conventional wisdom demands that principals take the heat for student achievement.

THE ACCESS EXPECTATION

The access expectation requires that principals be available to every parent, every citizen, every business leader, every politician, and on top of that everyone else who is in that school's community. Not only do principals have to be available; they are also expected to listen, to try to implement the suggestions (or demands) of these constituents, and to provide some evidence back to the public that their wishes have been fulfilled. Remember, the school systems in most nations, and especially in the United States, are democratic systems in which there are often publicly elected officials who have some major say in the administration of schools. School systems are also largely locally funded, meaning that the voice of even the least of the taxpayers is a booming voice that must be answered if not obeyed.

American school principals are unique compared to those of similar status and responsibility in other organizations because of the character of schools as a public service as well as publicly funded organizations. Schools are sometimes compared to hospitals for their degree of public permeation, but in reality these comparisons are woefully off course. While there is indeed quite a large degree of public penetration into health care, the public's ability to directly influence hospital decision-making is weak in comparison to the public's influence on schools.

Schools are organizations whose "clients" are generally the entire population of a nation or community. Schools are mass public institutions, meaning that every person has the opportunity (or right) to take advantage of this organization's services. Schooling is also compulsory in the United States and in many of the world's educational systems. So, not only does every person have the right to be schooled; everyone is also required to do so. This is dramatically different from health care organizations or hospitals, in which there is no daily requirement to get a checkup or complete a series of health tests.

Schools are the only organizations in the world in which high degrees of organizational autonomy and high levels of external penetration are both expected and required. This public access and performance accountability make the principal's job one of public service, but also one of complex contexts. This is quite the double punch, and it means that school principals, as the individuals at the top of their school's organizational chart, are double punched as well.

THE ACCOUNTABILITY EXPECTATION

The accountability expectation requires that the responsibility for the ever-increasing achievement or productivity in a school belongs to the principal first and foremost, and if ever the achievement expectation should not be met, then the principal must be doing something wrong.

The history of schooling in the United States is replete with calls for both accountability standards and standardization of the curriculum. Because American school principals are organizationally removed from the individual students and the technical outcomes of student learning (namely, student achievement), it may be argued that it is inappropriate to hold them directly accountable for these outcomes. Yet this direct accountability continues a long-standing appreciation among the education policy and reform community for the corporate structure and system of top down management with its accompanying accountability structure.

In an effort to ameliorate achievement disparities in the United States in particular, some educational reformers have also called for the standardization of curriculum and instruction. Standardization is often interpreted to mean consistency, rigor, and appropriateness of curriculum and instruction. But level of standardization may also refer to the administrative centralization of decision-making, because as content and standards become more consistent they also tend to become more centralized at increasingly higher administrative levels. Rising centralization of decision-making supposedly lifts the burden of curriculum and instruction from the subjective authority of principals. In other words, school principals' behaviors change and influence teacher instruction and student achievement differently as the level of centralization of decision-making changes.

Debates over accountability standards and centralization of decision-making have been the foundation for a mixed bag of research and policy regarding the influence of educational leaders on instructional improvement. Surprisingly, this debate has been limited largely to the United States. Because the United States has such a diverse educational system consisting of approximately 15,000 autonomous school systems (i.e., districts), researchers have had a hard time pinning down the extent of the relationship between school principals and student learning. They have not, however, had a hard time writing volume after volume about the assumed or expected relationship between leadership and instruction, even though the relationship is never fully or finally explained.

Questions about principals have been limited mostly to assumptions that principals always act rationally and consciously. To consider this dilemma about "leadership" and "instruction," two contrasting perspectives have been invoked. A conventional perspective predicts an association between variation in school principals' behaviors and variation in student learning. Other perspectives suggest that widely accepted models of school principal behavior may result from conventional reasoning, but the predicted outcomes of "school leadership" (such as student learning and achievement) may defy conventional expectations. For example, when student learning improves, it may not necessarily be because school principals' behaviors changed or precipitated the change. School principals may influence organizational-level change without any accompanying change in outcome at the student level. Similarly, differences in the observed behaviors and activities of school principals at different schools and in different school systems are not necessarily associated with changes in student learning.

For example, in schools where overall student achievement is average, this average score may not be representative of the whole student population at that school. There may be some high-performing students, some low-performing, and some performing in between. The average of the scores for the school looks mediocre, but in actuality there may be one group in particular that is scoring far above the norm. Similarly, there may be another group that scores quite low. What do principals do in this situation? Can they claim that high student achievement is a result of their behavior or activities in support of instruction and learning? If principals do make this claim, then what do they say about the extremely low-performing group of students at that same school? The simple variation in performance that occurs within one school makes the connection between what school principals do and how students perform tenuous at best.

Principals may not be accountable for student (or school) performance because the environment in which students live and learn, which is not a result of either schooling or instruction, largely influences this performance. School-level policies, decisions, and changes follow legitimate, rationalized models that exist as much because of habit or tradition as because they are effective in changing student performance. It is more appropriate to look at characteristics of a school's environment than to expect school principals to individually do or say things that improve school and student performance.

The nonconventional approach suggests that principals' individual resources and decision-making authority are not as significant to student learning as the institutionalized model or organizational context in which their behaviors exist and to which they conform. The school environment or type of educational system in which students and principals work may separate individual-level student learning from organizational-level school principal behavior.

Classic sociological works have argued that organizations like schools become structured by their environments and change with them (Meyer & Rowan, 1977). Of particular interest to school principals is the probability that cultural norms, which insinuate themselves across school organizations, disseminate through school principals' behaviors and activities. Rather than any sort of technical exchange between principals and students via principals' leadership behaviors and the consequences of their behavior, principals reflect organizational models applied to and shaped by school contexts.

Indeed, rational and contextually legitimate models of school structure, instructional processes, and institutional outcomes drive school
principals' behaviors. Legitimate principal behaviors depend on the institutional model adopted by each type of educational system. Variation
in school principals' behaviors should depend on the type of school environment in which they function. Variation in behavior that is contextualized to specific school conditions and communities should also be
more influential than behaviors that follow a strictly standardized
model. Differences in what school principals do in different schools
should reflect some common characteristics based on the system-wide
centralization of decision-making, but principals may still adjust what
they do to meet the expectations and needs of their local school environment as well.

A fancy way of saying this is that the level of centralization of
decision-making should influence school principals' ability to contextualize the instruction and learning that occurs within their schools. The
same institutional influences that contribute to the training, education,
and behavior of principals as rationalized and legitimate models of
school administration are products of the environment and preexisting
levels of student ability at least as much as they are causes of it. Principals in localized systems (as in the United States) can direct their behaviors more specifically to the contexts and situations of their schools
and students, theoretically leading to the provision of more appropriate
instructional resources and opportunities as well as optimal levels of
student learning.

There are several possible reasons why what principals do does not
directly influence student learning. One is that the prevailing legitimate
model for school principals' behavior is so strong that even when given
the latitude to influence instruction, principals do not take full advantage
of that opportunity and do not deviate significantly from the legitimate
model. Another explanation is that even when variation occurs, the legitimate model of school principals' behavior is so strong and the desire
for legitimacy so great that principals' behavior is not related specifically enough to schools' and students' contexts. One could also argue
that the transitory and temporary influence of principals cannot out-
weigh the consistent influences of resource and opportunity over the
course of students' whole academic careers. Yet even in the face of so

many reasons to doubt the impact of principals on individual student achievement, the push to hold principals accountable continues to grow.

Although schools become structured by their environments and change with them, what school principals do may be even further contextualized. Standardization of principal behavior through centralization of the educational system may not predict the specific decisions and behaviors of principals as much as the specific needs and histories of the schools and communities in which these principals are situated. School principals' ability to contextualize their behaviors and instruction within their schools is not related to student learning as much as to the organizational environment of their schools.

As seen in the example of Mr. Bowman, conventional perspectives afford too much significance to the standardization and accountability of school principals' behaviors when considering student learning. By questioning the conventional arguments that level of centralization of decision-making and emphasis of principal behavior should influence student learning and finding no significant relationships, some research has shown that the conventional arguments prevalent in both policy reform and effective schools circles are weak. Although qualitative and microlevel examples will undoubtedly continue to provide ample evidence of tight linkages between principal behavior and student learning, organizational-level investigations show that taking contextually situated instances and transforming them into broadly applied policy initiatives is ill-informed and ill-conceived.

When the chips started to fly over the knife on campus, the faculty and administration began polarizing over Mr. Bowman's personal policies. During my planning period one day I was summoned to Mr. Bowman's office. When I got there he sat me down and gave me a short talk justifying his actions. But what I remember most were his final words to me. He said that when parents came to him complaining about my teaching, he defended me. And in the current debate over his policy toward the student with the knife, he expected me to defend him. It was at that moment that I realized that Mr. Bowman was not the exemplary American school principal at all. He was the "boss" of our organization—nothing more. And in spite of his façade of "synergy" and "success," he was trying to run a small fiefdom, not manage a complex, democratically oriented, public organization.

The results of the achievement, access, and accountability expectations are definitely more than the sum of each part—but not in a positive way. When all of these expectations converge, the result is that school principals become victims of an accountability culture. They begin to believe the expectations and eventually resort to heavy-handed demagoguery.

CHAPTER 3

American Principals in a Global Context

Most of the published thinking on school principals focuses on uniquely American situations and concerns. This means that most of what is written about school principals is limited in scope and consequent generalizability. Nonetheless, internationally comparative perspectives are important because they encourage educators and policymakers to understand and consider the role of historical, social, cultural, political, and economic influences on educational development that may be unique to schooling in certain countries.

The few who have looked at school administration and principals from an international perspective have argued that "educational administration is highly resistant to internationalization" (Paige & Mestenhauser, 1999, pp. 500–501). This resistance is common among the school administration community, especially in the United States, where the myth of individual exceptionalism pervades the modern mass school system. One rationale behind this myth is that in such a localized system, the local administration of schools is specialized or tailored to the specific needs of each student, teacher, or school community. While these local adaptations do exist, they exist within the context of a larger educational system; in particular, a larger educational system that is based on the globally legitimized Western model of compulsory mass schooling.

In spite of the popular emphasis on American school principals and their uniquely American schools, there are many ways to look at schools and principals in the United States in light of other educational systems and achievements. Some of these points for comparison that influence national educational systems are the economics, politics, social demographics, and geography of a nation. The context for American school principals is unique because of the extremely localized nature of schooling. Some have argued that the localized nature of American schooling disadvantages American students in international comparisons of academic performance because of increased variability in students' opportunity to learn. It is this localization of schooling in the United States that creates most of the problems in comparing the United States with other nations. For example, some suggest that the United States is incomparable to other nations because of its lack of any national standard for teacher training or certification. Another important distinction between the United States and other nations is the high level of resource inequality between school districts in America.

Figure 2 shows the pros and cons of comparing school principals internationally. The pros of international comparison are that these sorts of comparisons can lead to appropriate contextualization of the conditions that influence school principals to behave and act the way they do. By looking at school principals in other systems of education, a standard can be established for evaluation of principals in the United States. Context and evaluation standards are two important reasons for internationally comparing school principals' activities.

One of the cons of comparing school principals internationally is that without proper understanding of the unique factors that contribute to each nation's school system and even each individual principal's school, the comparison can be one of apples and oranges. There is the danger that the comparison will be meaningless because of the fundamental differences in the systems and principals themselves. Another

Contextualization		Apples and Oranges
Pros	International Comparisons of Schools	Cons
Establish Standards for Evaluation		Ranking without Understanding

Figure 2. The Pros and Cons of International Comparison.

con of comparing school principals internationally is that the behaviors and activities of school principals may be ranked by nation and the rankings taken at face value without an accompanying understanding of what those rankings really mean or whether they really are important.

Regardless of whether international comparison of schools is right or wrong, Americans do it anyway—and have for decades. It is important to learn how to do it appropriately and to situate the American school principal crisis in a global context.

THE GLOBAL CONTEXT OF SCHOOLING

Many who study education believe that it was not until the 1980s federal report *A Nation at Risk* that the overall evaluation of the quality of American education was put directly into an internationally comparative context. Nothing could be further from the truth. The history of education in the United States shows that international comparisons have been a staple of the social, political, and economic agenda regarding schools since the establishment of the United States of America. It was not, however, until the mid-twentieth century that the defining rhetoric for American educational reform became one of national competition and a sense that America's economic future in the world is directly tied to the United States' educational success at home.

International educational comparisons result from an underlying assumption that the nation encourages and directs the growth of public schooling as a tool for creating productivity and citizenship (Fuller & Rubinson, 1992). Right or wrong, decades of such rhetoric pump up public interest in how American education compares internationally. Since international comparisons often promise to shed light on current social, political, or economic concerns, there is a sense that situating American education in a global context will inform Americans about what the nation should be doing with its schools. This same logic applies to international comparisons of school principals.

One of the great thinkers of the twentieth century, Alex Inkeles (1974, 1979), made a rather convincing argument that schools are contexts for modernization. This perspective seemed validated in the 1980s, when the countries that ranked high in international student achievement were also the countries with the highest economic productivity or growth. Yet as the 1990s progressed, and the highest scoring nations began slipping economically, this rationale was called into question. For example, Japan, which is typically one of the highest scoring nations in math and science achievement, experienced severe economic setbacks throughout the 1990s. Japan's economic woes were even more interesting as the United States, a nation consistently ranked in the middle and lower range in international comparisons of student achievement, had one of its most prosperous periods of economic development during the same time period. The popular logic that schooling and academic performance can always coincide with economic productivity crumbled with the fall of Japanese and other high-scoring nations' economies.

Meanwhile, scholars and policymakers began arguing that international comparisons of educational systems guide educational policymakers to model school policies on incomparable systems of education. It was the educational version of the age-old apples and oranges argument. This is a dangerous use of internationally comparative data because the context of schooling is often as important or more important than the content. Important to this criticism of international comparisons of student achievement are historical and traditional characteristics of educational systems. One of the most interesting public debates along the line of educational context and developmental stage of education took place between David P. Baker and Ian Westbury in the early 1990s (Baker, 1993; Westbury, 1992, 1993). Their debate concentrated on the interpretation of student achievement rankings in the United States and Japan given the unique educational opportunities and curricula in each nation.

Other debates suggest that the background influences of students and education professionals are always such significant influences on students and their schooling that international differences among educational systems are unimportant. These arguments suggest that school policymakers should look at differences in students' family income and other social or cultural background indicators to predict the effectiveness or impact of schooling on students, rather than at specific individual outcomes such as achievement scores.

Linking back to the Baker-Westbury debate, comparative sociologist of education John W. Meyer and David P. Baker himself have said that achievement is not the cornerstone of comparison. If true, this is a valuable lesson for American educational policymakers to learn relative to principals. Meyer and Baker (1996, p. 126) say that there is "a large literature on the institutional structure of modern schooling [which] argues effectively that schools are more than technical organizations of achievement."

Schools are instead institutionalized organizations whose functions extend beyond the purely academic or economic. Most schools take on as one of their fundamental functions the creation and incorporation of students as citizens in largely democratic nations. Public schools are also venues for the translation of local culture and national education policy into the instruction and achievement of students. As managers of these schools, principals oversee and are accountable for these functions, which vary by both school and nation. This means that there is a lot of difference in what school principals do, but that it is difficult to determine trends in school principal activity.

All considerations of school principals' activity should take into account that principals are individuals operating within an organizational or institutional context. Although individual school principals are the ones whose activities are being defined and measured, these activities occur within the contexts of organizations and are usually meant to influence the structure and operation of organizations as much as individuals. There is a hierarchically nested relationship between individual school principals' activities, the structure and form of the schools these individuals head, and the organizational environments within which they work and function.

Principal activity is oriented more toward systemic and sectorial concerns than specific problems or regions, although "extensive local knowledge" cannot and should not be discounted. This suggests a managerial approach to understanding school principals. From a management perspective,

> Management skills are . . . less specific to particular problems, and more restricted to specific organizations and industrial sectors; deal with a succession of tasks in one system, rather than a series of discrete tasks occurring in separate locations; rest on a broad, diffuse knowledge base which includes extensive local knowledge. (Noordegraaf & Stewart, 2000, p. 434)

Given the pressing focus on school principals, this is a powerful assertion. The management perspective, when applied to school principals, suggests that their activity is not specific to particular problems of instruction and learning within individual schools, but is restricted to the concerns and situations of types of schools and schooling that exist within national educational systems.

Extensive local knowledge, which may include familiarity with the community and external as well as internal local school culture, is included in the rationale or considerations of principals. Their activity is based on a set of broad and diffuse core beliefs about the appropriate activity of school principals. The institutional embeddedness of school principals' activity deserves attention, especially when that activity occurs in the public sector.

The nature of school principals' activity goes beyond the specific schools in which principals are situated to encompass fields of organizations or ranges of organizations whose structures and purposes have been synthesized and scripted as part of an institutionalization process. This institutionalization of schooling structures, processes, and, in particular, school principals' activity suggests both the expansion of organizational boundaries and the importance of national systems in the study of institutionalized organizations such as schools. The conventional wisdom about school principals ignores the unique contexts that principals work in and instead focuses on a one-dimensional idea of what school principals do and how that activity should be evaluated. It is time to question the conventional wisdom.

QUESTIONING CONVENTIONAL WISDOM

Most principals are perfunctory. They do busywork that could be outsourced or done by hiring low-level specialists in maintenance, security, finance, scheduling, and other areas. Far from leading, most principals currently are hunkering down, obediently taking their cues from and doing whatever the superintendent tells them to do; just as the superintendent is doing what the school board tells him to do.

—Irving Buchen

Unfortunately, political reasoning guides most educational choices. . . . Oddly enough, politicians are hanging these choices on the hook of "accountability." . . . Accountability will take the form of test scores, even though we know that intelligence and learning are much broader and more complex concepts. . . . And last summer, the *New York Times* reported that the National Blue Ribbon Award for Outstanding Schools will be awarded based exclusively on— you guessed it—test scores.

—Kristin L. Droege

It is ridiculous to assert that principals are perfunctory, as Irving Buchen does, but this is a growing belief among many Americans. In response to this dissatisfaction, most of the books and articles published about principals suggest that principals must be *visionary leaders* or they might as well pack it in. There is a public expectation that principals should be the CEOs of their schools, that the buck stops on their desks, and that leading their school toward some sort of educational victory is the only option regardless of what "victory" actually means. These popular expectations assume that school principals are change agents in otherwise stagnant, under-performing institutions.

The fact of the matter is that this is only a partial truth. There are indeed principals who are visionary leaders, fully responsible and in control of every administrative action, instructional method, and achievement score that occurs under the roof of their school. There are principals that inspire their teachers, parents, and students to perform higher than they ever thought possible. There are outstanding principals who are change agents in schools across the United States and around the world, and it is important to know who these principals are, what they look like, and how they do what they do. These sorts of visionary, charismatic leaders are the rock stars of school administration, but they are certainly not the norm for school principals in any district, state, or nation.

If principals are something other than visionary, charismatic leaders of their schools and communities, are they also ineffective? If principals are not the CEOs of their schools, are they bad principals? Without "rock star" principals, do the teachers and students stop performing at high levels or not perform as well as they could have under a visionary, charismatic leader? The answer is a resounding NO. While there are places for leadership, vision, and charisma in school administration, the majority of good principals are good *managers* rather than leaders in the popular sense of the word.

Good principals are not the "chief" or the "president" of their schools. They are the lifeblood of their schools. They are the oil that greases the wheel. They are the reams of paper that fill the copy machine. They are the behind-the-scenes mediators who resolve disputes among teachers, students, and community. Quite frankly, some of the best principals are invisible, completely opposite of the CEO change agents envisioned by much of the public and ingrained into school administration researchers and educational policymakers.

Why are the "invisible" principals not talked about more? Because they do their jobs and make things run smoothly without needing a lot of attention, without climbing the organizational ladder, without micromanaging and without needing to wield unrestrained power and influence over their teachers and students. The "invisible" principal adopts a more managerial style of school administration. Principals who act as school managers are never the focus of high-profile discussions, made-for-TV movies, or special issues of leading professional journals because this style is not flashy. Principals who manage simply do their jobs as well as possible. It is through the invisible principals' diligent management that things happen, whether they as principals are "in charge" of the class, program, and people at school or not. But there are politics and accountability measures that must be dealt with, as Kristin Droege suggests.

Part 2 continues the work begun in Part 1 by critically questioning the conventional wisdom that lumps school principals in with corporate CEOs and private businesses in terms of performance expectations and governance structure. In so doing, Part 2 asks several questions:

- Are principals instructional leaders?
- Are principals accountable for school performance?
- Are principals public servants or private executives?

The honest answers to these questions are not in line with the conventional wisdom. But by honestly answering these questions, principals in the United States just might find the tools to transition from heavy-handed leaders to democratic managers, or avoid the crisis entirely.

CHAPTER 4

The Leadership Dilemma

The allure of "leadership" is strong. Typical American school princi-pals rarely consider themselves visionary or charismatic leaders, yet they often aspire to be, even against their own better judgment. Why? The answer is easy to understand. School principals aspire to be vi-sionary, charismatic leaders because they are persuaded by the count-less voices in popular books and articles. The speakers and sessions at professional conferences persuade them. They are persuaded by the ex-pectations of everyone from the teachers and students at their own schools to the administrative officials at the district and national levels who tell them they should be these visionary leaders.

Conventional school leadership wisdom is a version of prosperity preaching. The logic is that if principals act a certain way, success will follow. For example, here are some of the latest titles of books being marketed to school principals and the higher education faculty who train them:

- *Lead, Follow, or Get Out of the Way*
- *The Moral Imperative of School Leadership*
- *Leading Every Day*

The catalogue taglines for these books are:

- "Why the principal should be seen as the COO (chief operating of-ficer) of a school."

- "Why the role of the principal should figure more prominently within the system."
- "Motivate your staff to work hard and stay focused on school improvement and student learning."

The fact is that school principals are rarely encouraged to be good *managers* because the leadership gurus have labeled management as weak and ineffectual. The facts suggest quite the opposite. The truth of the matter is that the majority of good school principals *are* good managers, but good management does not happen all by itself.

The nature of managerial work is slippery (Hannaway, 1989). And because of the expectation that school principals will be visionary leaders and inspiring agents of change, principals have a tough job wherever they are. There are pressures from parents, from business and community leaders, from school board members, and from state education policymakers, among others. There are pressures from national standards boards and committees, too. Principals are caught in the middle between what the public thinks about schools and what the reality of schooling is.

In an era of standards and accountability in schooling, and amid the preponderance of advice and commentary from every direction both inside and outside of a principal's school, how should principals do their jobs? Should they lead or should they manage? Are the two mutually exclusive or do they overlap? If school principals choose to manage instead of lead, how should they manage the administrative functions of their schools? And if they focus on administrative tasks, how should they manage the instructional functions of their schools? If principals focus on administration and either instruction or student achievement suffers, they are held responsible. If principals focus on instruction and learning but go over budget or ignore the parents that call every day, they are responsible. In a world of leadership expectations, how can principals "win" when they *manage* instead of *lead*?

As schooling becomes and remains the predominant formal mechanism through which citizens are formed, socialized, and prepared for adult life, the governance of schools becomes increasingly important. The pressure from parents, communities, and policymakers on principals to influence and, it is hoped, raise the achievement levels of students is significant. At the same time, the pressure to remain publicly accessible while fulfilling the leadership role is not only great but also inescapable anywhere schooling is universal and compulsory.

The idea behind conventional school leadership wisdom is that principals are dominant change agents. There is an assumption among the public and policymakers alike that principals can make a difference if they do, say, or support the right things. In particular, the conventional wisdom suggests that principals can shape the direction their schools take through a careful presentation of and firm conviction in their attitude, beliefs, and charismatic behavior. Each of these ideas has been carefully crafted to mimic the popular leadership approach geared toward the business executive and aspiring salesman found in books by well-known authors like Steven Covey with high-profile titles like *The Seven Habits of Highly Successful People*.

As we walk through each of these ideas, it is important to remember that in spite of the allure of these ideas, schools are still public, democratic institutions and not profit-seeking, private corporations. The difference is significant because the levels of public penetration that are possible in the daily operations of a school are vastly greater than those of any other institution.

ATTITUDES, BELIEFS, AND CHARISMA

The right attitude can move mountains, or so the conventional wisdom suggests. With a "can do" outlook and the suggestion of the well-known Hawthorne Effect at the ready to squelch doubters, the idea that attitude shapes achievement is consistently popular. The attitude approach suggests that the way the school principal acts affects the way the rest of the school acts, teachers and students alike. This is a staple of the conventional leadership wisdom and has been popular in business-related how-to books for many years. Dale Carnegie's successful *How to Win Friends and Influence People* books and seminars are a perennial example.

A fairly common saying among educators is that high expectations lead to high performance. There is research to support the validity of this statement. For example, the Hawthorne Effect just mentioned is the standard evidence used to support the attitude assertion of school leadership literature geared toward any level, not just school principals.

This example comes from a study conducted in an early twentieth-century factory. The researchers were investigating the effects of change in the workplace on productivity. They found, for example, that when they improved the lighting in the work area, productivity went up. When they came back and made the lighting worse, productivity still went up. The researchers found that the workers were responding to the fact that they were being given attention, not to whether the change in conditions was positive or negative.

Using the logic exemplified by the Hawthorne Effect, many educational reformers and policymakers have suggested that if principals have a positive vision for the school, teachers, and students, and they communicate this vision to the teachers and students, then their schools will perform at the highest levels.

The principle underlying the conventional wisdom about attitude is that school principals should pose for effect. They should present a way of thinking about what the goals of school organizations are and how everyone in the organization is going to work toward those goals. School principals should present this way of thinking in clear and un-ambiguous terms to the teachers and students most importantly, but also to the community and other stakeholders who may influence the direction a school takes.

There are right attitudes and wrong attitudes according to popular understanding. A right attitude is one that is change oriented, prominent, and focused on progress of some sort. A wrong attitude is anything else — meaning that a wrong attitude is one that is not change oriented, not prominent, and not focused on progress. Where are all of the good principals, who maintain the good that goes on in their schools, going to fall in this right and wrong dichotomy? If there is nothing broken, does it need to be fixed? If there is something that needs to be fixed in a school, is prominent, progress-minded change the only way to fix it? The obvious answer to both of these dilemmas is no, because again there is the underlying assumption of the conventional attitude argument. This assumption is that schools need change because either the school or the school system is failing. But as we have already seen, the truth about American schools is that they are doing better with every passing decade.

Another trend in the popular school leadership literature is that a principal's beliefs can change the climate and "success" of a school.

This is sometimes also called "vision sharing." By setting the tone through attitude, principals are said to be able to effect change in the whole school organization by laying down a set of beliefs. This can take the shape of a mission statement or philosophy, but whatever it is called the idea is that if everyone in the school shares the same positive goals, then these goals will be achieved and even spread the sort of psychological buy-in to the community that is necessary to make vision sharing viable for schools. There are scores of books and articles that suggest that principals should create a vision for the school that is shared by everyone in the organization.

The attitude that school principals present to their teachers, students, and parents has to be seen as the truth by those people. Everyone connected to the school should believe what the mission statement or officially stated goals of the school are as determined by the school principal. This is a leadership snafu in most cases because belief is not something that can generally be forced—unless the teachers, students, and parents already believe the primary underlying assumption, which is that there is something that needs to be fixed in the school or system and that the only way to do that is through the force of a school principal's character or charisma.

Charisma is one of the more intangible of the leadership traits that conventional wisdom often prescribes for principals. Because of its elusiveness, charisma is also one of the most sought-after leadership attributes of school principals. The concept that the person at the top (or near the top) of any organization's hierarchy pyramid should be charismatic is well known both in and out of school administration circles. Charisma is that magical property that makes one principal a leader whose every word is a nugget of wisdom and another principal a loser whose own teachers will not listen (much less the students), even if these two principals say and do the exact same things.

The charismatic school principal is the one whom teachers and students look to for guidance. This principal does not have to force anyone to believe the mission or goals of the school. The charismatic principal has a personal appeal or power to fascinate students and teachers, which by itself is enough to engender their loyalty and support. Charisma is the elusive characteristic that most school leadership discussions try to define and harness. It is a fruitless quest for many school principals, however, because charisma is not something that can be boiled down into five easy-to-learn lessons on leadership. It is something that someone either has or does not have. Fortunately and in spite of the conventional wisdom, charisma is not necessary to be a good school principal.

Consider the types of activities and behaviors that most school principals are expected to display. Principals certainly have administrative duty and instructional responsibility, but where does most of the influence on student learning and performance lie? It lies with the teachers, because they are the school representatives with the most daily direct contact with the primary "clients" of the school organization: students. Even if principals could influence instruction leading to learning, it will typically be through the way that they manage their schools to encourage or allow teachers to do their jobs to the best of their ability and students to the best of theirs.

Arguing that school principals are managers often does not resonate well with the principals, policymakers, and public who want to put their faith and trust in a clearly identified leader who is going to triumphantly take them "out of the wilderness" and into the promised land of educational equity and excellence. It may be the most realistic, and it may be based on empirical evidence, but management without the allure of leadership is not sexy.

If principals are not the visionary, charismatic leaders that the conventional wisdom advocates, what are they? Clearly, there are no school systems comprised entirely of visionary leaders. School principals are primarily managers. Management does not have the ring or allure of "leadership," but it is closer to reality. What do principals do that makes them managers more than leaders? Consider this: Do principals lead schools anywhere? Are they really agents of change? Or are teacher–student interactions in classrooms really where the rubber hits the road?

Leaders are individuals who chart new territory and inspire people to do things they would not ordinarily do. Managers make sure that organizations run smoothly, that resources are available, and that those they manage are able to do the jobs that they do best. Managers are support personnel; they are not CEOs or presidents, and least of all are they dictators. The word *manager* does not have the ring that *leader* does, and it may seem like a dull concept to those used to thinking about school principals in more romantic ways, but thinking of principals as organizational managers is an idea that may save schools by averting the crisis of heavy-handed leadership among school principals.

As mentioned earlier, Thomas Sergiovanni wrote one of the more influential books on school administration in recent history. In his book are many concepts and ideas that are both groundbreaking and part of a classic understanding of school administration. The idea of leadership is replete among Sergiovanni's arguments even though contextualizing that leadership is one of the aims of his text. The mere mention of leadership is not automatically a falsification of what school principals really do, but to suggest that it is the bulk of what principals do, and especially of what "successful" principals do, is not right. Part of the problem leading to the American school principal crisis is that much of the conventional wisdom looks at what "experts" would like principals to do or be like rather than closely examining what school principals are and how that understanding can improve the teaching and learning that is supposedly the goal of schools in the first place. No amount of wishful thinking is going to make American school principals something they are not.

If indeed we are honest, much of what principals really do can be called bureaucratic administration. The bureaucratic administration of formal organizations is an important phenomenon and is by no means unique to discussions of schools or instructional leadership. How white-collar bureaucratic organizations like schools are managed is and has historically been of particular importance to school principals. Prescriptions for administrative as well as managerial activity are widely debated and discussed both in and out of the educational community. Within these debates, there are rich discussions of various relationships between managerial activity and organizational output. This means that special attention has been given to the influence of managerial activities on school outputs like academic achievement and the "quality" of school graduates.

The concept of managing in a democratic bureaucracy is often thought of as something relegated to discussions of political science, but that is not the case at all. School principals are organizational managers in publicly permeable, democratic organizations. This makes school principals the most unique and misunderstood managers in any of the professions.

Like it or not, principals are part of a bureaucracy. Whether the negative connotations of that role become real or not depends on each principal's management style and school context. So what can they do about it? How do principals handle this sort of situation? The fact of the matter is that principals are stuck in the middle. Their bureaucratic dilemma is how to manage an organization that depends on the performance of others (students) while creating an environment in which all of the efforts of the organization are directed toward and contribute to that performance. This is a much more difficult job than many business executives confront. If the goal were to produce a certain kind of teaching, that would be much easier than trying to influence student learning and performance. Output that comes from those working as part of the organization is much easier to control than output that comes from the clients of that organization.

Because school principals do not have direct or in some cases even indirect influence on the accepted performance output of the organization they manage, the connection between what principals do and how schools perform is at best questionable. Yet for many years now it has been popular to equate school administration and performance with administrative styles and performance expectations of the corporate world. It was believed that what schools needed was more streamlining in their bureaucratic structure, leading to efficient, effective decision-making. This was the conventional wisdom regarding schools and their principals for most of the twentieth century. And gauging by the recommendations in books and journals targeting school principals, the conventional leadership wisdom continues to dominate discussions of school administration in the twenty-first century.

CHAPTER 5

Are Principals Instructional Leaders?

Most principals in the United States do not teach. Many began their careers in education as classroom teachers, but for reasons of status or salary found themselves sitting behind principals' desks. Yet principals are still expected to be the leaders of instruction at their schools. If principals are instructional leaders then everything they do should somehow influence the classroom instruction that students receive in their schools everyday. If principals are not instructional leaders they may still influence instruction, but it does not become their defining characteristic.

There are two movements in school administration that have become and continue to be widely recognized as setting the standard for school administrators, especially principals, beginning in the latter part of the twentieth century and continuing into the twenty-first. These two movements are related in that both assert the prominence of school principals as instructional leaders.

First is the Effective Schools Movement, which concentrates on the behaviors, actions, and methods of instruction that are supposedly the most "effective." In most instances, effectiveness is measured by average student achievement scores and gains in those scores. The second movement is the Accountability Movement, which is still a prominent reform movement and policy agenda in the early twenty-first century. The Accountability Movement almost exclusively uses average student achievement or average gains in achievement to measure school "success" and evaluate the impact or ineffectiveness of education professionals and school principals, in particular. Because these two movements are related, and in many ways causally related, it is important to first understand the

Effective Schools Movement and its impact on school principals, which then leads into or becomes the Accountability Movement.

Without rehashing the history of education in the United States, it is important to look at the Effective Schools Movement and its impact on (1) ideas about school administration in the United States and (2) how these ideas spread out and were interpreted in other educational systems at both the local and national levels. Foremost among the influences contributing to the Effective Schools Movement is the conventional wisdom connecting school administration with a corporate administration model. In the early twentieth century, progressive school reformers popularized this idea as a way to streamline decision-making and schooling processes that had become either excessively bureaucratic or politically corrupt.

The Effective Schools Movement accompanied a resurgence of corporate involvement in and comparisons to schooling. Most notably, the resurgence of interest in a corporate model of governance in the 1980s returned to an educational agenda that had not been so strongly emphasized since the early part of the twentieth century.

The linear development of reforms and school improvement movements in the United States that has impacted school principals is quite striking. Although the connections to school reform extend back before the beginning of the twentieth century, since 1900 there have been three broad reform eras as shown in figure 3. These eras have largely focused on (1) social, political, and economic progress within the United States; (2) comparison between the United States and other nations; and (3) performance accountability that combines internal improvement with external comparison.

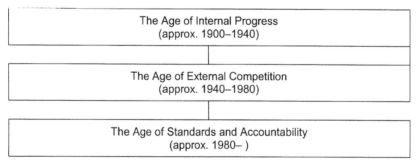

Figure 3.   *Timeline of Reforms and Movements Affecting American School Principals Since 1900.*

The Age of Internal Progress in American schooling roughly coincides with the Progressive Era of American history. The Progressive Era, which most scholars date from around 1890 to around 1940, was a period of reform in the United States that encompassed much more than the educational system, as any historian will explain, but the unique elements of the Progressive Era in the development of schooling in the United States make it one of the most transformative periods in American school history. Although there is debate about when the Progressive Era actually ended, if it ever did, there is fairly consistent agreement about the factors that collided to create the progressive movement in America: industrialization, immigration, and urbanization (Tozer, Violas, & Senese, 2002). During this time school principals came under scrutiny for political as well as economic reasons, although the social progress focus influenced each of these reasons.

School principals during the Age of Internal Progress of school reform in American history were criticized for their lack of efficiency and organization. These same principals were also given the task of engendering social, political, and economic progress within the United States. A popular solution was for principals to follow the corporate model of school governance. This idea was most prominently put into practice with the establishment of district superintendents who were to be the CEOs of the school district, but school principals, as next in line, were also subjected to this reform ideology and expected to follow suit.

The logic behind this push for corporate imitation was that schools were wasteful and bureaucratic. Conventional wisdom at the time suggested that if schools were headed by individuals capable of making executive decisions without having to work through a maze of bureaucratic approval, then more would get done administratively as well as instructionally. Another selling point for making school principals more like corporate executives was that they should be able to subvert bureaucracy to implement the best and most effective methods of instruction as soon as possible. This way students would not be bogged down in the bureaucratic mess that schools had largely become, especially in urban American centers.

Politically, schools were places that people believed could be used to alleviate the corruption that was rampant in urban areas in the United States. As immigrants flooded into the United States it was common for them to be herded by less-than-respectable groups or individuals into neighborhoods and, by association, schools that supported one political party or another. These affiliations were often defined by nationality or language, but all victimized the poor and uneducated. Schools then were used in these cases to indoctrinate and in many ways politically and economically enslave the populations that attended them. By creating a system that was more like a business model, the political corruption of the old system could be eradicated, it was believed, and a new era of schooling could emerge. School principals, as the heads of their schools, were often expected to take the lead in these reforms.

During the early twentieth century's Age of Internal Progress, social programs and curricula made the most inroads into schooling that they have made since. In particular, ability tracking or streaming was seen as a groundbreaking educational method during this period. The idea was that schooling should be tailored to meet the specific needs of individual students. This meant that students who were more "able" or likely to become, for example, mechanics were provided an education that emphasized the knowledge and skills necessary to be a good mechanic.

Students who were blessed intellectually were given a college preparatory education. Other social programs that provided for the nonacademic needs of students were also incorporated into schooling during this time. These programs may have been related to etiquette training (for female students), work programs for the economically disadvantaged, or meal provisions for those who needed food. While this era signaled a great leap in the philanthropic character of American society, the institutionalization of social programs in schools created a legacy of individualization and expanded accountability that continues to hound school principals.

Following the Age of Internal Progress, the Age of External Competition was barely underway as the United States entered the Cold War. At this time the emphasis in schools went from internal progress in the social, political, and economic arenas to an external academic comparison with other nations and their school systems. In particular, the United States pitted itself against the Soviet Union, and every aspect of this comparison was mirrored in the American schooling system. From the alteration of the Pledge of Allegiance to include the phrase "one nation, under God" as a daily school ritual to vicious rivalry in educational achievement and access, especially when it came to the areas of math and science, the Age of External Competition was a time for extreme external comparison. This focus on international comparison created a legacy of expanded accountability and competition for principals to deal with that has become a permanent part of schooling and educational policymaking.

In particular, one Cold War event spurred more policy debate and support for schooling than any other. This momentous event was the Soviet launch of the Sputnik satellite in 1957. Sputnik was a result of the race to space between the United States and the Soviet Union, and it became a small victory for the Soviets since they were the first to launch. This loss of face in the international competition between the capitalist, democratic world represented by the United States and the communist world represented by the Soviet Union led to an educational uproar. The defeat in the space race made its way back into criticism of the American educational system. The argument was that the American school system was not producing enough math and science experts to support the space program and other technical or military operations that might be necessary to repel or defeat the communist Soviets.

As a result of Sputnik, the U.S. Congress passed federal legislation allocating funding specifically for mathematics and science education curriculum development and program funding. This official turn to schooling at the federal level as a solution to international political competition signaled the reemergence of official reports and policy statements that overtly referred to schooling specifically as a means for national development. External comparison as a result of the Cold War is a significant influence contributing to the ongoing comparison of the American educational system and student performance with the systems and students from other nations. The Trends in International Mathematics and Science Study (TIMSS) is an example of this ongoing national education comparison and the degree to which this schooling comparison has been institutionalized as a method of national political and economic legitimization both in the United States and around the world.

The impact on principals of this Age of External Competition is that they are held accountable not only for the progress and performance of their individual schools and students but also for the degree of progress and performance in comparison to other nations, some of which have extremely different social, political, and economic environments for and approaches to society and schooling. Inevitably, American school principals are asked to compare their schools and students to the performance and progress of the schools and students in the highest performing nations in the world.

The Age of Standards and Accountability follows closely on the heels of both the Age of Internal Progress and the Age of External Competition because accountability movements require that school principals take responsibility for both internal progress and external competition. Schools and students are expected to improve significantly according to standards set by educational policymakers. They are also expected to rank higher in comparisons of achievement and progress between schools, states, and nations.

Part of the reason for this collision of reform eras in the Age of Standards and Accountability is that once a system of school reform and "improvement" is put in place it is nearly impossible to remove it from the institutionalized programs and structure of schools. This ideology also becomes a part of the conventional wisdom because it is ingrained into the general public consciousness of those who grew up hearing the dogma of whatever reform movement was popular during their youth. For instance, there is a generation of youth who believe that the American school system is failing and that higher standards and stricter accountability are the only way to salvage it, in spite of the fact that most of these same youth are attending college and going on to become prosperous in the social, political, and economic arenas of American life. It was during the time of transition from the Age of External Comparison to the Age of Standards and Accountability that the Effective Schools Movement officially came to life.

Beginning around 1980, the "effective schools" and "standards and accountability" movements in the United States began to reincarnate the early twentieth-century arguments that schools are organizations in which knowledge and skills are technically blended and delivered to each school's "customers." This overtly rational (and largely economic) technical metaphor was not, as mentioned, new, nor was it to end with this movement.

Rather than limiting these arguments to the United States, the Effective Schools Movement expanded these notions of performance accountability across American schools, school districts, and to other nations as well. The Effective Schools Movement also gave birth to the notion of principals as instructional leaders as much as or more than bureaucratic administrative managers. In assessing the effectiveness of American educators, including school principals, the Effective Schools Movement also expanded the focus of systematic evaluation beyond the United States to include comparisons with other nations, most notably Japan.

In his study of effective school research from a Japanese perspective, Kazuo Kuroda (1995) found that Japanese schools could be characterized by several effective schools traits. Japanese schools (1) focus on student acquisition of central learning, (2) use appropriate monitoring of student progress, (3) hold high, operationalized expectations for students, (4) provide a productive school climate, (5) encourage salient parent involvement, and (6) provide practice-oriented staff development. Kuroda suggests that the effectiveness of Japanese schools is due to cultural and societal characteristics that over time infiltrated the school system and replicated the "effective" characteristics that so many in the United States admire. The most interesting finding of Kuroda's study was that the only difference between Japanese schools and the ideal effective school is that Japanese principals play a limited leadership role.

In their role as "instructional leaders," American principals frequently have been expected to manage their schools in a way that emphasizes activities that enhance or benefit classroom instruction and learning. Although there is no more specific or consistent definition of instructional leadership than this, the expectations are that principals will for the most part either directly or indirectly influence how teachers instruct their students and how students learn from their teachers. This may mean that principals could be expected to spend most of their time demonstrating model lessons for teachers, providing adequate professional development time for teachers, or even making sure that students enter their classrooms "ready to learn." Regardless of the specific activity, the "bottom line" is that students post high achievement scores as a result of what principals do. Whether looking for a "bottom line" in schools is appropriate or not is never really questioned from the effective schools perspective.

Throughout the 1980s and 1990s, educational policymakers, scholars, and practitioners seized upon the notion of principals as instructional leaders and simultaneously deemphasized principals' roles as managers of highly penetrable formal organizations. The driving rationale behind most school management and educational administration higher education programs is that "effective" school managers have broad effects on instructional quality and school or student performance. Instructional leadership in many nations, including the United States, is evaluated and measured in general terms such as school output, accountability, standards, rigor, and economic impact, particularly in studies conducted as part of the Effective Schools Movement.

Even among practicing educators and other school professionals, there is a popular assumption in America that principals are in positions of authority and responsibility to affect and mold the formal structure of instruction at their schools. The popular belief is that through their station in the organizational hierarchy, school principals can facilitate and encourage the production of effective instruction leading to high student achievement. The conventional wisdom is that principals are in positions of "instructional leadership" by which they can influence student performance levels, even if they do not always take advantage of that opportunity.

Four expected activities of principals, which are representative of instructional leadership perspectives, are (1) developing mission and goals, (2) managing the educational production function, (3) promoting an academic learning climate, and (4) developing a supportive work environment (Murphy, 1990). The instructional leadership argument says that these dimensions relate either directly or indirectly to school outputs such as student achievement, each with a positive result.

According to this instructional leadership perspective, when principals develop mission statements and goals they influence school output because the substance of instruction is molded and shaped by the ideological foundation of the school in which it occurs. A school's technical outcomes are motivated and determined by its intentions. The belief is that by creating rigorous and academically encouraging goals and objectives, instruction will follow suit and inspire high levels of student achievement.

In schools without educationally influential missions and goals, teachers and other school personnel cannot or will not have the direction nor the ideological resources to teach well and inspire high performance. A continuation of this argument suggests that by unifying the educational vision for a school, principals can harness the collective power of ideological and philosophical inspirations that otherwise occur among teachers in relative isolation. Much of the instructional leadership approach suggests that principals' creation, support, and reinforcement of school mission and goal statements influences schools' output and effectiveness.

The argument that principals manage student achievement suggests that principals significantly influence what teachers do in their classrooms and how students receive their instruction. Curriculum and instruction specialists assert that the key to student learning is the method or process of instruction and instructional management itself. It is important from the instructional leadership perspective to understand that principals control and direct the many components and resources contributing to the process of instructional implementation. In this role, principals are responsible for giving teachers and others with direct student contact the necessary resources and opportunities for quality instruction leading to high performance. This could be done through in-school professional development, instructional modeling, or constructive criticism and evaluation situations.

Another way of thinking about how principals manage instruction is to think of principals promoting an academic learning climate that emphasizes the immediate environment in which teachers instruct and students learn. In order to promote an academic learning climate, principals need to create situations in which the only concerns are learning and performance. Immediate environments should have as many resources available as possible, thereby giving students and teachers many opportunities to productively interact. Rather than directing what students or teachers do during instruction (the process), these principal activities direct what students and teachers have available to them (the resources) throughout whatever instruction and learning situations arise.

If principals develop a supportive work environment they extend the immediate and available environment of resources, thereby focusing on teachers and students more directly. An essential element of this category of instructional influence is the interaction and peer development among individual teachers. Regardless of student performance or activity, principals are often expected to provide material resources and professional development opportunities, and to spawn peer support networks among teachers as well. Although it may be difficult to direct this sort of teacher-to-teacher interaction, it is expected that principals will create and encourage these peer relationships and on-the-job support networks. The instructional leadership perspective suggests that principals' support for and provision of material resources, professional development opportunities, and peer interaction among teachers influences schools' output and effectiveness.

By focusing on how principals manipulate school ideology and structure, instructional process, immediate environment and local context, and resource support, an instructional leadership approach asserts that principals can influence student achievement by promoting the best and most appropriate teacher instruction at every schooling stage and situation. And in spite of analyses suggesting the opposite, there is a major strand in the educational community of scholars that argues that principals are connected with school output. It is this strand that is most frequently cited by educational policymakers.

Instructional leadership proponents largely ignore the impact of school environment on principals, although they emphasize principals' responsibility to manipulate the environment. Unfortunately, measuring principals in light of schools' organizational environments has been inconsistent from study to study. In spite of this inconsistency, instructional leadership advocates in the educational research and policymaking communities continue to focus on specific instructional leadership activities of principals.

ACHIEVEMENT ENVY

Underlying the Effective Schools Movement and conceptions of instructional leadership is "achievement envy" at all levels of schooling. "Achievement envy" is a product of the market-driven ideology that permeates most Western institutions, including schools, as indicated in figure 4. There are several assumptions that coincide to create achievement envy.

The first achievement assumption is that progress is the result of positive change. This means that the only way to track or measure progress in schools is through increases in or high levels of performance, which is typically defined as student achievement. This assumption is based on the capitalistic, market-driven economic ideology that is the basis for many of the core beliefs in Western and particularly American institutions. In a more basic economic sense, the assumption that progress is the result of positive change might refer to profit or other

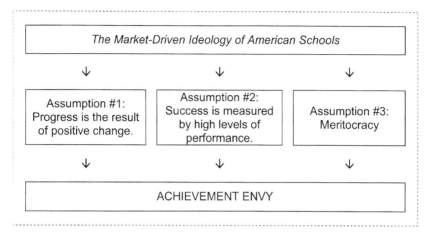

Figure 4.   *The Context and Assumptions Leading to Achievement Envy.*

resource accumulation in business ventures. In the schooling sense, this assumption states that the only good that can come out of schooling is high or increasing student achievement scores. This first assumption is the source of achievement in "achievement envy."

The second achievement assumption is that high levels of perform-ance measure success. This assumption is similar to the first, but fun-damentally different because the emphasis is on the value of the per-formance rather than the characteristics of it. To claim something has been a "success" if the output or result is high performance sets the stage for comparison. How else will those who evaluate know what is "successful" and what is not unless they have compared performance between schools or educational systems? By comparing achievement levels in an institutional context that values market-driven change and change leading to profit, in particular, this second assumption is the source of the envy in "achievement envy." Comparisons of educational systems and the school principals within those systems focus on stu-dent achievement as the primary indicator of "success."

The third achievement assumption is that schools operate within the boundaries of a meritocratic system. This is a strong foundation of the American educational system and of other educational systems that have either been based on the American model (or other Western mod-els) or have borrowed heavily from the American school system (or

Western models). A meritocracy is a system in which individuals earn what they have or achieve based on their own efforts (or merit) rather than as a result of aristocratic privilege or some other form of non-merit-based gain. The idea that achievement is earned and deserved means that when performance levels are stagnant or low, especially in comparison to other schools or school systems that the public or policymakers feel should not be outperforming the school or system in question, achievement envy sets in. This sort of situation is interpreted through a meritocratic lens as being the result of laziness or a lack of effort on the part of those in the school—the students, teachers, and especially the school principal.

The conventional concepts of effective instructional leaders thrive on achievement envy. The school principal becomes the vehicle for fulfilling the desire for high levels of positive achievement gain through harder work and more efficient schooling. Instructional leadership is both a product of and a supposed antidote for achievement envy. Yet instructional leadership, for all of its common sense and sincerity, is not really an effective way to improve instruction or achievement because it often focuses more on the "leadership" than the "instruction" aspect of school principals and what they do in schools.

In spite of its popularity and tremendous impact on school principals, the instructional leadership perspective is fundamentally flawed when it comes to research on school principals. First, a significant amount of the published research samples on the dependent variables of high levels of school and student performance. This means that studies purporting to "prove" the effectiveness or success of "instructional leaders" usually stack the deck by selecting only the best examples to be in their studies. Most studies of this sort completely ignore the great mass of principals either succeeding without being instructional leaders or failing miserably while presenting the ideal image of an instructional leader.

Second, those that sample more widely tend to ignore the multilevel nature of schools' organizational environments when conducting analyses. In other words, they claim to show that principals who are instructional leaders somehow improve student achievement or some other important school outcome while ignoring the many other influences in students' homes, their communities, or in the general schooling atmosphere that have nothing to do with principals as instructional leaders and everything to do with why student achievement is high.

Third, the published research focuses almost exclusively on the United States, Canada, and the United Kingdom, meaning that there are relatively few internationally comparative or international analyses of principals. Contextualized international comparisons are considered less frequently in educational policy research than in other policy research agendas, even though international comparisons often drive policy reform agendas for schooling, particularly in the decades following the Age of External Competition.

Research on principals, particularly the research used to form educational policy, does not often emphasize the importance of school context. Rarely do studies explore alternative perspectives concerning principals' activities and organizational environment, especially when comparing school principals' behaviors and activities across schools and educational systems. This pressure on principals from parents, communities, and policymakers to influence and raise the quality of student instruction is more of a popular accountability movement than a research-based agenda. Yet the activity of educational administrators, such as school principals, in the United States is difficult to prescribe since each school, district, or system is potentially unique.

The main problem with the instructional leadership approach to principals is that there is no consistent evidence that principals are indeed responsible for the academic performance of schools, namely, student achievement. Nor does the instructional leadership perspective provide an empirical method for directly measuring, estimating, or evaluating the oft-assumed but rarely observed relationship between what principals do and student achievement. There is not sufficient empirical evidence to show how principals accommodate contradictory or otherwise complex school environments and still are connected to student learning enough to have a measurable effect on student achievement.

Do school principals impact individual student achievement? The emphasis of the instructional leadership approach is that principals proactively shape or determine school and student performance, but a more reasonable approach suggests that principals "re-act" more than they "pro-act." If instead of actively influencing student achievement school principals are spending most of their time solving problems as they arise, then the "proactive" argument is weakened and the "reactive" explanation for school principals' behavior becomes more plausible. Unfortunately for Effective Schools Movement and instructional leadership proponents, it is difficult to hold school principals accountable for student achievement if their behavior is largely reactive instead of proactive.

During the 1980s, there was specific pressure from the educational research and policy communities for principals to emphasize activities that would enhance or benefit classroom instruction and learning. This has often meant that, as managers of organizations whose formal or official functions are instruction and learning, principals are responsible and accountable for school outputs such as student achievement. In particular, instructional leadership proponents suggest that school principals are the most effective of all potential instructional leaders because they are situated within schools (unlike district or regional superintendents) but not embedded so deeply as to be overwhelmed (as teachers can be) by students' individual characteristics.

In the 1990s, a distinct but complementary effective schools approach emerged that emphasized transformational leadership and organizational learning and was grounded more firmly in the empirical study of organizations. This counter-movement asserted that schools are learning organizations, and thus principals' main objectives are to facilitate and guide student learning and classroom instruction rather than overtly direct learning and instruction. These arguments suggest that principals accomplish "transformational leadership" by fostering teachers' autonomous development of good instructional practices rather than by telling them how or requiring them to do so. This facilitation or guidance, according to the "organizational learning" approach to transformational leadership, comes largely from providing teachers and students with whatever tools are necessary to instruct and learn, respectively, without principals directing the process themselves. In particular, the organizational learning perspective focuses on variation in school situations and communities.

The period of the most significant debate between these two effective schools approaches to school principals' instructional leadership activity (the late 1980s and early 1990s) was also the period which saw the most empirical study of the influence of principals' instructional leadership activity on student achievement. In fact, during the late 1980s and early 1990s the emphasis on school effectiveness and the blossoming of the school effectiveness ideology may have led to an enthusiasm in the published research for predicting a significant positive influence of principals on student achievement where there was indeed none. This unique phenomenon in the published research suggests that positive and significant effects of principals' activities on student achievement may have been the products of trendy interpretation rather than reality.

There are also contradictory explanations for the impact of principals between the more traditional instructional leadership proponents and the organizational learning proponents. The instructional leadership position, which suggests that principals overtly manage and are individually accountable for school outputs because of their position relative to local school needs and conditions, is unreasonable according to organizational learning proponents precisely because every school has unique students, teachers, parents, and other situational and community variables. The organizational learning perspective suggests that variation between school communities and situations is the reason why principals cannot direct the development of "best instructional practice" (and school effectiveness as measured by student achievement).

Instructional leadership is the answer most frequently and vehemently given for why school principals do what they do, but empirical evidence of this is rare. A seminal study, which lends empirical credibility to the instructional leadership position in light of the organizational learning alternative, was published by Ronald Heck, T. J. Larsen, and George A. Marcoulides in 1990. In this research article, the authors claim not only to empirically measure principals' activities but also to show that these activities are positively related to student achievement. Heck, Larsen, and Marcoulides claim that principals are indeed instructional leaders (although they do not use this term) in that their activities are associated with student achievement and that certain activities are positively associated with achievement.

Heck, Larsen, and Marcoulides suggest that the relationship between principals' instructional leadership and student achievement is causal rather than coincidental. This means that their study claims to present conclusive empirical evidence of the effects of principals' instructional leadership activity on the primary output of instruction, namely student achievement. This is an important argument. If the relationship is causal, then policymakers and training experts should emphasize the benefits and qualities of certain instructional leadership activities. In addition, public stakeholders such as parents and community members should assign responsibility for student achievement to principals and other administrators higher up in the schooling hierarchy. The problem is that other empirical studies report little or no influence of principals' instructional leadership activity on student achievement.

If "effective" principals are indeed accountable for the performance of students in their schools, then empirical research should be able to conclusively determine whether or not principals' instructional leadership activity influences school effectiveness. There is much evidence to suggest that there is no direct relationship and that even the indirect relationships between what school principals do and how students perform is weak. The instructional leadership and administrative policy reform advocates still assert that principals can and do influence school effectiveness, in general, and student achievement, in particular. Why is this?

Such inconsistency in empirical research on the relationship between what principals do and student performance leads to further unanswered questions. If principals do not solely behave in order to affect student performance—or, at least, since their efforts to do so are inconsistent— why then do principals do what they do? Is there any relationship between variation in principal activity and variation in school environment? If so, is this relationship due to unique school situations or community variation, as the organizational learning approach suggests?

SITUATING SCHOOL PRINCIPALS

Schools are academic learning centers, social meeting and socialization venues, and community centers for the education and training of a society's young. Yet each society has unique characteristics, and each community within each society has special needs and concerns. This is especially true when the context varies across nations as well as within nations. With these sorts of layered characteristics, needs, and concerns, is it fair to say that principals in all schools should behave or act in the same way? Are there certain core administrative duties that principals must perform in all schools before customizing their activity for their particular school? In this era of globalization and international citizenship, why have few policymakers or public representatives expanded the concept of school community to include national- or international-level contexts as well?

There is significantly more research on principals' instructional leadership activity coming out of English-speaking, Western, developed nations than out of other nations. This presents a problem for understanding why there is a uniquely American school principal crisis. As already mentioned, in the United States, as in many Western nations, a culture of individual rights and responsibilities permeates most organizations, and social or public organizations such as schools in particular. This is a crucial point for understanding the predicament that American school principals are in because this notion of individualism goes beyond individual rights to embody the notion of individual responsibility as well. Along with these individual rights also comes the responsibility not only for oneself, but also for those one has assumed responsibility for through "leadership" roles. The notion or expectation of individual principals' responsibility for the processes and products of schools is a defining element of American school principal accountability.

Accountability itself can be defined as expectations of responsibility for and authority over activities and performance. The notion of individual school principals' accountability for school performance and output is prevalent in American discussions of educational policy and reform, where expectations are typically high, even at the national level. There is also the element of accountability to the stakeholders and constituents that make up the specifically American environments around schools. There is a lot of discussion about the need for accountability and what it should look like, but little discussion about what accountability actually does to principals. Seldom do Americans consider the effects of accountability on principals.

Administrative roles and systems for political, justice, and business organizations are not as permeable or publicly penetrable as those in the mass schooling model, which is standard in most developed as well as developing national systems of education. As compulsory public social organizations with arguably the most diverse as well as inclusive array of stakeholders, publicly derived funding, and difficulty in evaluating the service provided, American schools and those who manage them are expected and increasingly required to answer not just to their immediate "customers" (i.e., students and their parents) but to communities and other organizations at the local, regional, and national levels as well.

For instance, parents of students from any background or social class may not only meet with school personnel, such as superintendents, principals, and teachers, but they may also demand that their children receive particular treatment or that school programs be administered in a particular way. In many communities, parents are even asked to serve on decision-making committees that affect the ways that schools are run and the education that students receive. The permeability of operation is also one of the biggest causes of the strict and massive public accountability to which American schooling officials, and especially school administrators such as principals, are subject.

The formal accountability system in American education becomes a ceremony predicated on the school effectiveness rationale, which perpetuates the myth of a positive and significant relationship between what principals do and student achievement. The American accountability ceremony for principals is both followed and celebrated as a way of legitimizing schools as learning institutions as well as vehicles for social, political, and economic development. Student achievement, being the most widespread and measurable indicator of school effectiveness, becomes the object of these accountability ceremonies. So the myth of the relationship between principals' activity and school effectiveness becomes more important than actual empirical evidence of any relationship between the two.

CHAPTER 6

Are Principals Accountable for School Performance?

Where does the buck stop? If principals are expected to influence student achievement, then it is natural that they would be expected to be accountable for the performance of students and their schools in general. This school accountability trend has strong ties to economic policies and productivity levels in the United States. One way the accountability trend manifests itself economically in relation to schools is through school-to-work transition policies, agendas, and programs in schools.

There is a prominent American education policy point of view that making schools accountable to businesses and communities improves individual students' academic performances. This point of view can be tested by looking at the association between the amount of influence that businesses and other community stakeholders have on schools and either the level of, or gain in, student achievement. Some of the public discussion in America about this economic-educational accountability system even uses Japanese and German school-to-work transition models as evidence to support this point of view. The resulting conventional wisdom is that the more influence business and community stakeholders have on schools, the better students will perform.

School principals are held accountable as the heads of their schools for students' transitions from school to the job market, even though economic conditions may have nothing to do with the appropriateness or content of what students learn and do in school. This popular connection between school principals, student performance, and students' future economic productivity is often made to highlight the importance of school principal accountability.

Although expectations for and assumptions about principals' activities are or are becoming relatively standardized across schools and school systems around the world, the modern mass education system has deep roots in the United States and is largely based on capitalist economic assumptions. The early twentieth century's Age of Internal Progress in the United States coincided with the advent of scientific management based on the ideas of Frederick Winslow Taylor and the "invention" of mass production techniques by, most notably, Henry Ford.

Educational reformers in the early twentieth century in the United States were enamored with the scientific method. In business and industry, the emphasis on scientific management and mass production techniques led to individual workers becoming unknown and faceless but simultaneously more efficient and effective. These changes not only affected the nature of producer–consumer relations and the economy but also altered the nature of school–student relations in general and the nature of the principals' job in particular.

By applying scientific management principles to schooling, educational reform during the Age of Internal Progress and since has involved, among other things, the belief that the technical process of schooling can be understood and better run through quantification and categorization. The scientific method was accompanied by the idea of social efficiency for school reformers. This meant that there was a belief that society could also be quantified, categorized, and "understood" so that it would run smoothly (like a "well-oiled machine"). Principals, as the heads of these educational factories (i.e., schools), were responsible for creating and maintaining an efficient and effective system of educational production for the benefit of society.

Capitalist Americans in the twentieth century understood how businesses operated and they applied this understanding of business and industry to schools, assuming that one organization is like another. There was a push by reformers to replicate the corporate model of governance in schools. Although done with good intentions, in hindsight, treating public schools like businesses was and continues to be a mistake, which makes the continued connection between school and business in the twenty-first century even more surprising. The reasons for this connection are relatively straightforward.

Before, during, and since the early twentieth century, American schools have been bureaucratically administered formal organizations. As such, schools and their principals have historically drawn much criticism for not generating the most productive students in the most efficient and effective ways possible. One early example, highlighted in a much-debated critique of school reform in the United States written by David C. Berliner and Bruce J. Biddle (1995), came in 1912 when public schools were lambasted in the *Ladies' Home Journal*:

> "[Can you] imagine a more grossly stupid, a more genuinely asinine system tenaciously persisted in to the fearful detriment of over seventeen million children and at a cost to you of over four-hundred and three million dollars each year—a system that not only is absolutely ineffective in its results, but also actually harmful in that it throws every year ninety-three out of every one hundred children into the world of action absolutely unfitted for even the simplest tasks of life?

The American hatred of bureaucracy, and simultaneous propensity for creating it, has ensured this continual criticism of schools as bureaucratic organizations. The bureaucratic expansion of schools and the subsequent criticism of this bureaucracy were partly due, during the twentieth century, to tremendous growth in public school attendance. This growth in attendance was largely due to the influx of rural dwellers into urban areas and also to the large numbers of immigrants coming to live in American cities during the late nineteenth and early twentieth centuries.

The solution to bureaucracy in America has typically been to streamline administrative procedures. In American society, one of the more popular ways to streamline administrative procedures is to adopt a corporate model of governance in which there are clearly recognized hierarchies of authority and decision-making. As discussed in chapter 5, the corporate model of school governance suggests that there should be one "executive" head in charge of larger districts with the power to streamline and empower the educational process and, more importantly, with the responsibility for doing so.

School principals were and still are expected to be executive leaders who are ultimately accountable for the output of their schools and students the same way that the business leader or executive was and is traditionally expected to be accountable for the bottom line (although recent critics of business involvement in education have highlighted the hypocrisy of such an artificially black-and-white view of the corporate model of school governance and accountability).

At the same time that twentieth-century educational reformers were extolling the virtues of a corporate model of school governance, they saw the development of a strong, vocal middle class in the United States and the shift of schooling from a *privilege* to a *right* to a *requirement*. With this shift in social consciousness and the increasing mobility of the poor to rise and become part of the middle class, schools also became institutions for social change rather than strictly academic institutions (Ravitch, 2000).

This also meant, of course, that school administrators such as principals were beginning to be held accountable for issues larger than the transmission of knowledge to students. The very future of society was believed to hinge upon the success or failure of schools to educate students. To twentieth-century school reformers, schooling became such that principals as schools' executive heads were touchstones for the rise and demise of American society, public welfare, and, more specifically and importantly, political and economic conditions. This perspective persists into the early twenty-first century.

WHY PRINCIPALS ARE NOT CEOS, COOS, OR CFOS

Why not see the school as a businesslike organization and the principal as the CEO, COO, CFO, or some other kind of chief officer? Well, there are several important differences between how a business operates and how a school operates. First, think about the goals of a business. There are several types of organizations. Some well-known types of organizations are membership, ownership, client, and public-at-large (Blau & Scott, 1962; M. Droege, 2001).

Membership organizations work toward the mutual benefit of those involved in them. Examples of membership organizations are fraternities and sororities, because these are comprised of individuals seeking to help each other. Membership organizations often operate under conditions of broad, internal control. Ownership organizations are typically businesses like General Motors that operate under the assumption that the CEO or president can make and enforce policy without consulting those individuals who work there. Ownership organizations operate on the principle of efficiency. Client organizations are mostly professional service organizations like law firms. These organizations are driven by the client (e.g., the client's need) and operate to produce excellence. But none of these types of organizations describes what schools do.

Finally, there are the public-at-large organizations, which are characterized by their contribution to the common improvement of society. These organizations are represented by government institutions because of their universal access and public-good characteristics. Public-at-large organizations are operated under broad, external control, which, it is important to point out, is not necessarily internal, efficient, or excellent. According to this definition, schools are public-at-large organizations. The organizational distinction of schools from other types of organizations is important for school principals.

Principals' activities in schools are unique compared to those of executives in other organizations because of the character of schools as both public service and publicly funded organizations. Principals must manage their schools according to local school community contexts and immediate needs while also considering and responding to national educational goals, trends, and expectations for schooling.

What principals do may be a response to school-level needs, national-level expectations, or both. Each of these levels of needs and expectations may be called an organizational environment. At each level, these organizational environments are characterized by varying levels of complexity. Complexity in organizational environments is largely a product of the number of stakeholders, needs, or expectations focused on the organization in question, namely, schools.

A complex school-level organizational environment would be one in which principals have many different interest groups or educational stakeholders involved in administrative and instructional decision-making. There are not clear boundaries between different levels of schools' organizational environments because the levels are both overlapping and nested, meaning that schools' local communities and contexts are situated within national systems of education and national contexts for educational accountability and expectations (see figure 1 in chapter 1). This nesting and mixing of environmental influences occurs in spite of traditional boundaries such as are politically defined as distinct districts and states. This combination of complexity within and between levels of schools' organizational environments may be one of the most significant elements determining principals' activity.

Managerial activity, which has over the years been broadly defined as literally every activity engaged in as a part of an individual's role as manager of a particular organization, is largely a response to the characteristics of the organization itself and the organizational environment. Therefore, school principals' activities are determined by the school community and context.

School principals' activity is also an example of the relationship between educational policy and its intended effect. The relationship of local or school-level policy on instruction is influenced by both the intended and unintended effects of principals and provides a microcosm of the relationship, if any, between organizational norms and organizational output. With increasing consistency, student achievement reports and comparisons at both the national and international levels drive educational policies and declarations. In the Age of Standards and Accountability, these policy statements and declarations often target the structure, methods, and rigor of subnational (i.e., state and local) educational systems rather than the available material resources and opportunities to learn.

Evidence suggests that the association of school principals' activity with a school's organizational output, such as student performance, has been and continues to be particularly weak in spite of increasing pressure to standardize and regulate this relationship. School principals dedicate more time and resources to legitimizing the processes and consequences of schooling than to improving the technical output of instruction. By focusing on school legitimacy the range of school principal activities is becoming increasingly normalized.

APPROACHES TO ACCOUNTABILITY

There are predominantly three ways to answer the question of whether school principals are accountable for school performance. The first and most popular is the instructional leadership perspective described in chapter 5, which suggests that principals do what they do in order to effect change in student instruction and achievement as well as in other school outcomes such as enrollment control and so forth. From this perspective, school principals are indeed accountable for school performance because there is a link between what school principals do and what students learn. The link may be direct or indirect, weak or strong, but as long as a link exists between what school principals do and student achievement, holding school principals accountable for student achievement is appropriate.

A second approach suggests that what principals do is largely a response to the characteristics of the school organization itself and its environment rather than a result of school principals' individual initiatives. For example, since schools are fundamentally educational organizations dedicated to either improving, maintaining, or discussing student learning, principals' activities are often related to either improving, maintaining, or discussing student learning and achievement. One difference between this approach and the instructional leadership approach is that school principals are oriented toward meeting the needs of the school organization rather than toward an isolated goal such as high student achievement.

From this more organizational perspective, however, school principals are still accountable for school performance because again there is a link between what principals do and how well or to what degree students perform. The difference between the rationales of the instructional leadership and organizations perspectives is that from an instructional leadership perspective principals' behavior is assumed to be predominantly based on rational choice and to be proactive. In the organizations perspective, principal activity is assumed to be predominantly contextualized and responsive, but again somewhat subject to rational choice. The common factor in the instructional leadership and organizations perspectives is that in both the activity of school principals is intended and expected to relate to student achievement levels. The timing or sequence of the proactive instructional leadership behavior may be different from responsive, organizationally contextualized principal behavior, but both suggest that changes in school principal behavior associate with changes in student and school performance.

Another way to look at principal accountability rejects the instructional leadership and organizations assumptions. This third perspective suggests that principals do what they do because of institutionalized norms for principal behavior and activity. Principals' activities may contradict these norms in response to local needs and environmental pressures. From this perspective, school principals cannot be held accountable for school or student performance because school principals' behavior and activity have no association or relationship to school performance.

School principals do what they do because they follow legitimized scripts or models for school principal behavior, not because they intend or expect to effect change in either the school organization, teacher behavior, or student learning. This does not mean that school principals are mindless drones acting without regard for local needs or circumstances. On the contrary, this approach suggests that the behavior and activity of school principals is nested within and limited by the legitimate norms and expectations for that school's, district's, state's, and nation's educational system (see, again, figure 1 in chapter 1).

In spite of this debate about why school principals do what they do and the validity of holding them accountable for school performance based on their actions, most of the public and educational policymaking community ascribes to the adage that the buck has to stop somewhere. As the publicly recognized heads of schools, principals are held accountable for school performance regardless of their real influence on school performance.

THE INDIVIDUAL EXCEPTIONALISM OF SCHOOL PRINCIPALS

There is a unique concept in Western and, in particular, American society that has permeated institutions and organizations of all kinds, including schools. This concept is that of "individual exceptionalism." Individual exceptionalism is the idea that individual people are not only capable of exceptional behavior, but they are also able and expected to act independently and take responsibility for those actions. In American society, the concept of meritocracy is closely linked to individual exceptionalism because in a meritocracy individuals are expected to merit or earn whatever they achieve or receive.

School principals in the modern mass schooling system are subject to the rule of individual exceptionalism. School principals are expected to act independently in their role as school head. The outcomes of the organization they head (the school) are their sole responsibility as well. The accountability consequences of individual exceptionalism are extreme for school principals because of the public access to and involvement in schools. Because schools are mass, compulsory institutions, everyone or almost everyone is compelled to participate and perform in schools as a student.

School principals take individual responsibility for entire generations of youth at one time in their respective communities. Although individual exceptionalism is a strong concept, it is hardly reasonable to expect school principals to shoulder this sort of burden, yet they do so every day. As a result of the individual exceptionalism assumption in Western and particularly American society, accountability for the performance of schools and students can become a monkey on principals' backs.

Whenever the public or the government is involved in an organization, it is certain that there will be results accountability. Those in the for-profit world of business like to assert that they are accountable through profits and market-driven competition, and indeed they are. But nobody in business is accountable the way that educators, in general, and school principals, in particular, are accountable. The reason why is that in the for-profit business world there is tangible incentive for performance. If a business does well, there is a monetary profit that the CEO and others involved in the organization can claim. In the world of education, there is rarely tangible incentive. Educators of all walks, including school principals, are never going to be highly paid relative to other professionals. The most tangible incentive for school principals is an incentive to abandon education. If principals' schools show high performance or improvement, they may be offered lucrative positions outside of education in the for-profit sector.

Principals are held accountable for school performance even though they do not directly affect performance either of teachers or, more importantly, of students. Principals are held accountable even though there is little tangible incentive for them to affect performance in their schools. Principals are held accountable not just to their immediate supervisors, which in most cases are the district superintendents in the American system. Principals are held accountable by and to the general public.

Anyone and everyone has a right to question what principals do and how they do it because the educational system in many countries is like the American system, which is universally accessible and universally compulsory. Performance accountability becomes a burden because of the degree of access to schooling everywhere. This universal and compulsory access leads to a high level of public permeability and accountability in schools in the United States and anywhere else that this sort of access to schooling exists.

The word accountability has become the modern mantra of educational reformers, policymakers, and practitioners in the United States. Since the release of *A Nation at Risk* and as recently as No Child Left Behind, the emphasis on educational accountability has captured the attention of the public, school professionals, and policymakers alike. For example, the U.S. Department of Education (2002, p. 9) says

> The [No Child Left Behind] Act is designed to help all students meet high academic standards by requiring that states create annual assessments that measure what children know and can do in reading and math in grades 3 through 8. These tests, based on challenging state standards, will allow parents, educators, administrators, policymakers, and the general public to track the performance of every school in the nation.

As this statement demonstrates, American educational accountability is closely tied to an expectation of public access to schools and the ability of the general public to stand in judgment over schools. Educational accountability has been invoked as part of political campaigns and promised by school principals. By itself, accountability means little unless clear and uniformly accepted criteria are used to define it, yet there is no standardized school evaluation tool or procedure in the United States and a plan to introduce one (Voluntary National Tests during the Clinton administration) was soundly rejected by states and districts across America.

THE ACCOUNTABILITY MONKEY

In spite of the indefinite nature of school accountability, Americans believe in it. It is often equated with the "bottom line," which is the basis of market-driven business, and as part of a capitalist nation Americans understand that. The heavy reliance on student achievement scores as a measure of "success" has led to accountability being the "monkey" on principals' backs.

The accountability monkey is the false but widely held American assumption that schools and, in particular, their principals can affect and should be responsible for student achievement in spite of an absence of any clearly defined or uniform system for evaluating the performance of principals or schools. As figure 5 shows, the accountability monkey is fed by the three assumptions made possible by the public permeability of schools. These three assumptions are that (1) schools are like businesses, (2) principals are like CEOs, and (3) individual exceptionalism applies to principals. Even in the face of mounting evidence to the contrary, the accountability monkey will not get off American school principals' backs.

Up to this point, the word "causal" has been used sparingly. It is a dangerous word. It suggests that something or someone causes something to happen and can then be held responsible for it. What is worse is that it is embedded in a popular belief in "leadership" and the effects that leadership can have on those being led. To understand the enormity of causal assumptions in social science research is important as well. For example, to say in the research world that a causal relationship exists between two things means that there is evidence that can be seen, touched, tasted, or somehow observed that proves that one thing causes another to happen. This is a dangerous assumption when talking about school principals.

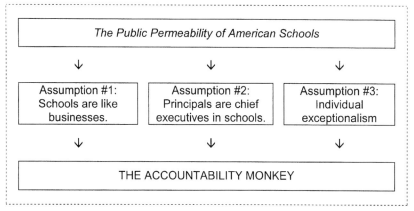

Figure 5.   The Context and Assumptions Leading to the Accountability Monkey.

The assumption has been made (and already criticized in chapter 5) that school principals "cause" performance at their schools to either go up or go down. There is no verifiable, replicable, or consistent evidence to support this causal assumption. More specifically defined, a causal assumption is an expectation that something (A) causes something else (B). It is usually a linear relationship, meaning that it goes directly from A to B, and it typically flows in one direction. So if A is school principal behavior and B is student performance, then the causal argument says that principal behavior (A) causes student performance (B). The results of causal assumptions are extreme accountability for the causal agent (i.e., school principals) and are usually accompanied by overwhelming interest in the outcome (i.e., school performance as measured by student achievement scores). The use of achievement testing as a way to gauge the quality of schooling is one consequence of causal assumptions.

The argument that school principals and student achievement are causally linked is an old one. It is fairly easy to argue that this causal assumption is false. But even with all of the evidence in the world, it is nearly impossible to change the popular attitude of school administrators and the general public that these two things are causally linked. Some have tried to make this causal assumption more palatable by saying that the relationship between school principals and student achievement is not a direct one but an indirect one. The idea is that by removing the direct causality, the argument becomes more valid. This is simply not true. The direct–indirect debate simply becomes a minor schism among otherwise tightly connected denominations of the same instructional leadership camp.

There are plausible arguments that when principals affect the instruction teachers provide in their classrooms, they have some sway over the student learning that occurs. But the idea that this impact on student learning shows up in assessments of student performance is still a mighty stretch. What about parents? What about peers? What about all of the thousands of little influences that affect students and how they perform that are not linked in any way to what principals do?

Then there is the argument that school performance as measured by student achievement is something that accrues over the course of many years. How well Suzy Student does on her state assessment is not the result of the instruction she received since Ms. Brown became her principal, but instead is the culmination of years of learning both in and out of school. The argument that learning is cumulative is a strong one, and it flies in the face of the assumption that school principals are causally linked to student achievement. What it does suggest is that there is a context or an environment in which learning and performance occur that not only is shaped by general performance levels in schools, but also shapes the way that principals behave.

So in a sense a causal link (albeit a weak one) may indeed exist, but this link goes in the wrong direction, meaning that the achievement environment of schools may determine in part how principals act rather than vice versa. This is the real shocker to most of the true believers in the causal link theory, but it is not an entirely surprising concept. It is similar to the organizations perspective discussed earlier. It also has elements of common sense. The nature-versus-nurture arguments of the developmental psychologists and sociologists have long debated whether people do what they do because they see an effect resulting from their actions or because they have been taught and expected to do it that way. The more interesting question asks, To what extent do school context, principal activity, and classroom instruction intersect?

As mentioned before, educational policy statements and accountability declarations often target the structures, methods, and rigor of state and local educational systems rather than the material resources and opportunities to learn that have been the foci of many educational research studies and reports in the latter half of the twentieth century. Much of the reason for this emphasis on structures, methods, and rigor rather than physical resources and opportunities results from studies that argue that although resources and opportunities are important, they are not as influential regarding student achievement as community and family influences are. Since the well-known Coleman Report of the 1960s, this finding has been repeatedly misconstrued to mean that school resources do not matter. American educational policy and scholarship often reinforce the notion that physical resources do not influence achievement as much as other factors.

Without resources as a primary influence on student achievement, policies responding to perceived "crises" of educational achievement target the structures, methods, and rigor of educational systems with particular emphasis on what principals do to "lead" their schools to "success." Yet more critical citizens ask whether this is really the heart of the concern over school achievement output.

Is educational structure causally and positively related to student achievement? Do the policy recommendations aimed at modifying or manipulating that structure at the school level really influence student achievement by regulating and enforcing the implementation of accountability policies for school principals? Are Americans more concerned with test scores than education in the broader sense? Are schools and principals really on the frontlines of this challenge? Or are families, communities, and other social institutions shirking their duties to school-aged children?

U.S. educational policymakers, whether working at the national, state, or local level, often ignore contextual variation and its influence on how principals behave. The bottom line is often student achievement regardless of context. Why? Because test scores are easily collected, compared, and understood by policymakers and the lay public, or so they believe. Administratively autonomous educational systems seldom are considered. Others have argued that state systems of education, although loosely federated through the U.S. Department of Education's curricular recommendations and selective funding, operate autonomously as independent administrative units. Yet, again, policy related to student achievement and principals' behavior is often meted out without reference to or regard for each school community's unique context.

Educational policymakers and school administrators frequently assume that there is a legitimate model for school administration and, specifically, "leadership" that transcends administrative or organizational boundaries. By extension, questions of school administration, leadership, and policy prescriptions should also extend beyond other traditional organizational and administrative boundaries.

According to popular American assumptions, the legitimacy of a standard school administration model applies across as well as within school districts and even national systems of education. What creates these American assumptions? What explanations for principal behavior do these assumptions suggest? Since principals do not directly influence student achievement through their behavior, why do they do the things they do?

CHAPTER 7

Are Principals Public Servants?

The public demands access to schools. As a result, the activities and behaviors of principals are unique compared to those of executive heads and lead supervisors in other organizations because of the public nature of schools. What does it mean for schools to be "public" institutions? The most important element of the public aspect of schools is the degree to which people and groups outside of the school can influence what happens inside the school.

If a group of people in a school district does not like the curriculum that a teacher teaches they can go to that teacher, the principal, or the school board and literally demand that the curriculum be changed. Good examples of this are the frequent disputes over the teaching of evolution as a fact versus theory (and the exclusion of the creation theory). When this becomes an issue, community members can and frequently do demand change. On a daily basis teachers are told or asked to adjust what and how they teach and principals are told or asked to adjust school policy. The public permeability of schools, especially in universal compulsory educational systems, is tremendous.

Principals must manage their schools according to local school community contexts and immediate needs while also considering and responding to national educational goals, trends, and expectations for schooling. The pressure on American principals to respond to external expectations is especially strong. Figure 6 represents the various stakeholders that middle school principals in the United States, Canada, Japan, and Germany say have a lot of influence over decisions made regarding their own school. The variation among nations regarding their reports of decision-making influences is large, but their similarities tell a story, too.

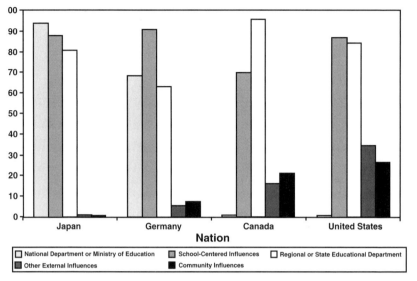

Figure 6. *Percent of School Principals in Japan, Germany, Canada, and the United States Reporting that Stakeholder Groups Influence Their Decision-Making "A Lot." Source: Third International Math & Science Study, 1999.*

As figure 6 shows, school principals in Japan and Germany report that their national ministries of education have a lot of influence over what decisions are made within the individual schools (roughly 95 and 70 percent, respectively). In Canada and the United States, national-level influence is practically zero. All four nations' school principals report relatively high levels of influence from the state or regional departments of education as well as school-centered influences.

There are about two to three different strong influences on decision-making within schools, and these pressures come from the national, regional state, and school administrative levels. Interestingly, community influences are strongest in the United States and weakest in Japan. Although these community influences are at their highest in the United States at approximately 25 percent, this is significantly higher than the community influences on school decision-making in Japan, which is about zero. The mix of influences and the various weight that is given (or taken) by each administrative level and organizational environment is tremendous even in stereotypically highly centralized educational systems like Japan. For example, more than 80 percent of the Japanese school principals surveyed report that the national, regional, and school level all strongly influence their decisions.

What principals do may be a response to school-level needs (students, teachers, parents, business and community leaders), national-level expectations (school boards, departments or ministries of education), or both. Each of these levels of needs and expectations may be called an "organizational environment." An "organizational environment" is the context in which an organization operates. This context influences not only the structure and function of the organization but also the activities and behaviors of individuals associated with the organization. School principals as either the literal or figurative heads of a school organization act within the unique context of their school's organizational environments.

At each level of decision-making, these organizational environments are characterized by varying levels of complexity. "Complexity" in organizational environments is largely a product of the number of stakeholders, needs, or expectations focused on the organization in question. A complex school-level organizational environment would be one in which principals had many different interest groups or stakeholders involved in decision-making. For example, the more that businesses, religious groups, parent associations, and other school community groups have a part in deciding what curriculum is taught to students in a particular school, the more complex the organizational environment of that school is. These sorts of complex environments for schools are more common in localized national educational systems, such as in the United States, where school penetration by outside interests is frequent.

A simple environment for schools would be one in which curricular decision-making was a function restricted to the centralized bureaucratic authority of a national ministry of education or similar entity, such as in France, where it is often joked that educational bureaucrats know exactly what each classroom across France is doing every hour of every day.

Complexity in schools' environments is not a function restricted solely to either the local or national organizational levels. This complexity can also be a product of the combined stakeholders, needs, and expectations for schools occurring at both the local school and national organizational levels. Complexity can occur both *within* single levels of schools' organizational environments (such as local and national) and as an interaction *between* these levels of organizational environment (Fletcher & Sabers, 1995). This "interaction effect" is an important concept in understanding the implications of a highly permeable public organization like schools. Schools in systems that have centralized goal- or standards-setting authority and localized implementation authority will be some of the most complex environments for schools because standards and expectations from the national level may both coincide and conflict with local-level needs and expectations.

Consider the effect on a school principal in a state that has implemented accountability policies regarding minimum achievement levels. These policies often state that principals at schools performing below a certain minimum may be terminated from their positions. Consider also the impact on these same principals at schools with consistently low-performing students. The behavior and activity of these principals is driven by student achievement and efforts to improve that achievement to the minimum required by the state because there is a conflict between the local-level environment of low achievement and the state-level organizational environment of high standards and accountability.

Consider also the interaction effect on a principal in the same state with the same high standards and accountability policies, but at a school that traditionally performs at the highest levels. In this situation the behavior and activities of the principal are going to be much different, although in both cases the principal's job is at stake. In each case the school principal's behavior and activities are influenced by the interaction between organizational environments, but with different effects. What school principals do is largely a response to the characteristics of the school as an organization itself and to the school's organizational environment rather than initiatives inspired by individual school principals' motives or the individual performances of principals. Within the instructional leadership and policy fields there is a common belief that a positive, causal relationship exists between what principals do and student performance, as if principals were acting to directly influence student achievement.

WHO CALLS THE SHOTS?

If school principals are going to be held accountable for school as well as individual student performance, they should at least have a clear idea of whom they have to answer to, right? Well, actually, wrong. In most organizational pyramids principals report primarily to district superintendents, but real life doesn't follow an organizational chart. There is a much more amorphous entity out there that keeps both the principal and the superintendent in check: the general public. This is a scary thought for school principals since the general public does not have a unified policy or opinion and often contradicts itself.

The general public is self-motivated at the individual level, meaning that what Citizen Q thinks is best and right for schools and school principals may be exactly the same as what Citizen X thinks or, and this is the scary part, it could not only be different from what Citizen Y thinks but also directly contradictory to Citizen Y's deeply held convictions about schooling. The truth is that school principals answer to everyone. In particular, they answer to the loudest and most persistent ones, who are often the ones with a grudge, an agenda, or a loose screw. This is the most extreme problem of access that any organizational head could imagine, but it is a defining characteristic of American school principals' daily lives.

Specifically, principals answer to stakeholders drawn from school administration and governance, school instruction and teaching, and the various social, political, and economic institutions and groups that exist among the general public. Figure 7 graphically illustrates the myriad of stakeholders that school principals answer to. What makes this a dynamic

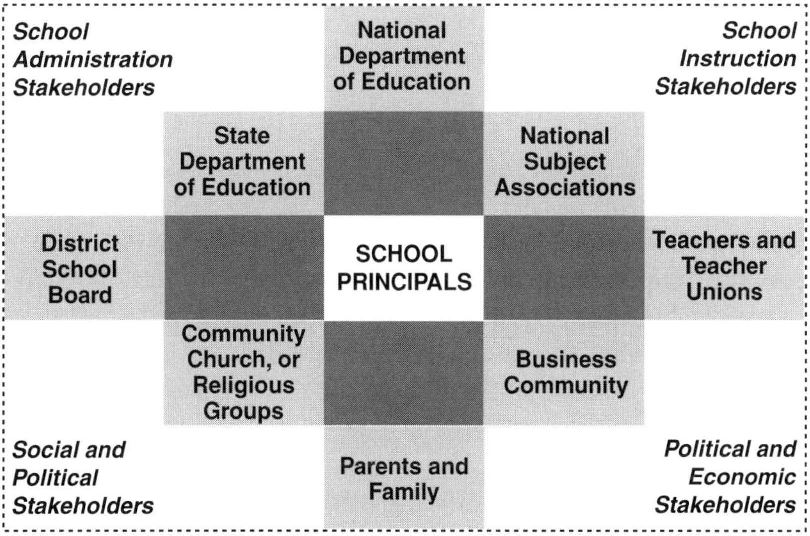

School Administration Stakeholders	National Department of Education		School Instruction Stakeholders
	State Department of Education	National Subject Associations	
District School Board		SCHOOL PRINCIPALS	Teachers and Teacher Unions
	Community Church, or Religious Groups	Business Community	
Social and Political Stakeholders	Parents and Family		Political and Economic Stakeholders

Figure 7. *Who Do Principals Answer To?*

yet possibly destructive conglomeration of stakeholders is that all or none of them could have the same convictions and agendas for schools and school principals.

In most instances, principals are simply a sounding board that individuals or representatives from each group can use to vent their frustrations with the system or make suggestions for improvement or change in the schools. The nature of the school principal's responsibility within school organizations is not such that each of these stakeholder's opinions and comments can be ignored. Because the United States has a public system of education, each of these stakeholders is a significant contributor and in some way "owns" the schools in their community. This makes everyone the superintendent, in a sense. Each individual citizen in the United States and other democratic nations with modern mass schooling systems expects the school principals in their community to be accountable to them for the performance and progress of their school's students and for overall school achievement.

If principals are not causally connected to student achievement, and if accountability for school performance is misplaced, why are principals the ones feeling the heat when a school's achievement scores drop or fail to reach "acceptable" standards? Who is really accountable? Whose responsibility is it to see that little Johnny and little Suzy learn and perform? Think about the context in which children grow up. Who are their models, mentors, and teachers? Does all or even most learning occur in schools or is there another institution, such as the family, community, church, or other social, political, or economic entity, that has more contact with and more influence on children?

Accountability for the youth in any nation might more appropriately rest on the shoulders of the family first, the community second, and other institutions third or even fourth before schools. But the nature of schooling assures that it is squarely on the shoulders of schools that responsibility and, as a result, accountability ultimately lie. Why? First, because schooling is, once again, a mass, compulsory institution. It is the most overt social, political, and economic requirement that any young citizen must complete. Everyone must go to school. There are laws that govern school attendance and prevent youth from doing other productive things like work or study without officially recognized supervision.

A second reason why schools and school principals are held firmly accountable for the achievement and social, political, and economic performance of youth is that the schools in the United States and many nations have extended their responsibility beyond that of simple academic education. As figure 7 suggests, schools have always served some social, political, or economic purpose beyond academic learning, but beginning in the twentieth century this additional responsibility was formally incorporated into the school system and structure itself.

School principals oversee nonacademic services geared toward the social and economic development of youth. Consider the role of administrators other than the school principal. For example, the school psychologist serves the emotional and other special nonacademic needs of students. The school counselor provides assistance to students as they transition to the world of work. As more and more nonacademic services become a part of schools and are overseen by school principals, the operation and structure of schooling becomes increasingly permeable by the public. The combination of universal and compulsory attendance with the assumption of services that extend beyond the classroom and into students' homes and families assures that the public in general feels entitled to have broad and unrestricted access to the schools and their principals. Accountability may be misplaced with school principals, but the reasons for this misplaced accountability are a consequence of the school system itself. Systemic conditions are hard to change, leaving little hope for change in the ideas of accountability for student learning and performance that plague school principals.

ACCESS ENTITLEMENT

One explanation for this misplaced accountability is a sense of entitlement to access created by the conditions and democratic assumptions of schooling. The predominant schooling model in the United States and around the globe is the modern mass schooling model. This model operates under explicitly democratic assumptions. As figure 8 shows, there are several conditions that contribute to a sense of access entitlement that are unique to this modern mass schooling system and result from these democratic assumptions.

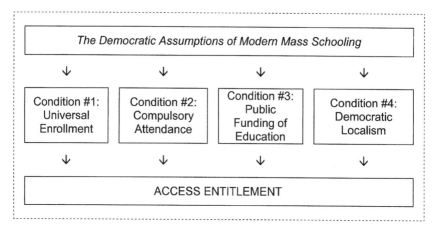

Figure 8.   *The Context and Assumptions Leading to Access Entitlement.*

The first condition for access entitlement is universal enrollment. It is a given in modern mass schooling systems that everyone of school age will be enrolled in the age-appropriate level of schooling and receive roughly the same prescribed content and instruction that educational policymakers have deemed appropriate for that system, school, and student. This condition contributes to access entitlement by establishing a familiarity with schooling and a belief that everyone knows what is best for schools because they have all been students for many of their formative years. Because of this universal school experience, the general public never feels shy about giving their opinion about schooling and expecting school principals to not only listen, but also act on their advice and recommendations.

Compulsory attendance is the second condition that contributes to access entitlement within the democratic context of modern mass schooling. By requiring that everyone of school age enroll in and attend this institution, there is a sense among the general public that they have "paid their dues" and that now the school system must serve their needs and, in some instances, whims. By compelling everyone to attend schools, the government, which usually administers schooling, is saying that schooling is more than a right, it is an obligation. The sense of obligation to schooling is then coupled to the notion that this obligation deserves reciprocity. Because everyone is required to attend schools as youth, everyone feels entitled to reenter schools as a "consultant" or "advisor" at any point in their adult life.

The third condition contributing to access entitlement is the public funding of education. As a government-related institution, schools are typically funded through public means, which usually means taxes. The public funding element means that every citizen who pays taxes has in some way supported the schools. This is also true of other government-related institutions such as the criminal justice system or the parks and recreation department, but because of the universal, compulsory aspects of schooling, there is a sense of entitlement that results from the public support of schools that is not mirrored in attitudes regarding other publicly funded institutions. Perhaps the sense of entitlement regarding other institutions would be just as strong if everyone were required to serve time in a prison, go to the park every day, or, as they do in some countries, enlist in the national military guard for a short period after high school graduation.

Public funding means that the public feels a sense of ownership not just through the fact that they spent a significant portion of their lives serving the institution of schooling as students, but that as they become adults they are required to again serve the institution financially through taxes. These conditions combine to create a strong sense of ownership of schooling and a strong, and in many ways justified, sense of access entitlement.

Democratic localism is the fourth and final condition that contributes to this sense of access entitlement. This is a condition that is unique to democratic societies and the United States in particular. Democratic localism is the conviction that local communities should govern themselves, whether the governance consists of political decisions regarding public law or policy decisions regarding public schools. For this reason, the district school board is a solid part of every American community's political system and often a springboard for individuals interested in pursuing political office at the state or national level.

The concept of democratic localism regarding schools holds that not only should a community's schools be governed by the local community, but the local community should have a strong and significant voice in the formation of relevant educational policy as well as the daily workings of its schools. It is a part of the larger democratic understanding in the United States and other democratic nations with modern mass schooling systems that individual citizens will be entitled to access to *their* schools at any point and time. The point of access or contact is, of course, the school principal most of the time because school principals are the most immediate school officials present and recognized at school board meetings. These school board meetings are the most probable place for the general public or citizenry to permeate the school organization because they are meant to be public forums where citizens of the community can come and air their complaints, praise, questions, or suggestions regarding the schools or a particular school in their community.

To summarize, the nature of schools is mass and compulsory in most nations, including the United States. This means that literally everyone is a stakeholder in the schools. The immediate "clients" (students and parents) are the eventual community at large. With so many stakeholders and so many points for the public at large to penetrate, reform, and generally mess around with schools, school environments become outrageously complex environments to work in, especially if you are a school principal.

So many stakeholders and points of penetration also means that school principals are under enormous pressure to satisfy everyone's needs. This pressure is intensified when stakeholders' interests conflict. The fact of the matter is that principals cannot please everyone all of the time, so prioritizing needs and stakeholder interests becomes a consuming task. Principals must constantly make political decisions about whose needs are more important based on the merit of the need itself as well as a bevy of other considerations, such as which action will not only appease the stakeholder in question but somehow pay off for the principal or school itself in the long run. There is no end to the repercussions that principals' decisions may have both for the principal as an individual and for the organization and those directly involved in the organization, particularly the teachers and students.

The behavior of principals as public servants is undoubtedly more complex than is captured here. The overriding principle is that principals' behaviors are a response to the amount of authority they are given to manage instruction and student output according to their schools' environmental contexts, rather than the other way around. This suggests that the standard instructional leadership arguments prevalent in the conventional wisdom are weak.

Variation in what principals do from school to school within the United States, as well as from system to system between nations, is a function of the complexity of yet another aspect of schools' organizational environments. There is a dual purpose of schools, which leads to further complexities and organizational conflict. In the highly charged, publicly permeable environments of schools, principals' behavior may be driven more by outside pressures for legitimacy than internal concerns for student achievement. This is not to say that technical output is not part of the environmental mix for schools or is not a concern of school principals. It just means that many other objectives occupy school principals' time and efforts, and these are often the result of the general public's expectations for achievement, accountability, and access.

The problems and pressures arising from public access and the multilevel and multipurpose conflicts inherent in schools' organizational environments are the source of the dilemma that has plagued school principals for decades. Are principals supposed to handle the situations that endlessly arise during the course of a day at school, or are they supposed to chart a path for their school toward a worthy goal? A common complaint among school principals in many nations is that they spend most of their time dealing with the little crises that constantly arise (i.e., putting out fires) and rarely have the time or the energy to shape comprehensive plans for the development or reform of their schools. Again, this can be seen as a consequence of context.

Depending on what sort of environment principals have to work with and in, they adjust their behavior and activity either toward daily crises or toward future planning. This, however, is not enough to curb the growing American school principal crisis. The reality of school principals' lives is that the short-term goals of "firefighting" overshadow long-term planning. Achievement, accountability, and access expectations consume principals so that often the only solution they see is to become increasingly heavy-handed. While this is certainly a fatal flaw, heavy-handedness immediately alleviates the pressures resulting from achievement, accountability, and access expectations. Of course, this immediate solution comes at the expense of long-term survival. The dilemma requires a change in the policies on, expectations for, and behaviors of school principals. But to make changes in the policies, expectations, and behaviors regarding school principals first requires a new way of thinking about principals.

PART 3

New Ways of Thinking about Principals

There is a patent irony in how school administration has conventionally been viewed. The influence of principals has been sought in overt forms of leadership and supervision, in kinds of relations presumably tied to their position of authority but whose effects do not readily penetrate the classroom door. Nowhere does this view recognize that the principal's significant influence lies in the allocation and shaping of the school's most basic resources: children's characteristics, learning materials, and time. But these influences are generally established, not in conspicuous social encounters, but in activities usually denigrated as clerical chores in which charts are filled in and names put to paper. These quiet influences, however, shape the conditions under which teachers work; they constrain the forms of instructional organization and influence learning indirectly yet powerfully.

—Rebecca Barr & Robert Dreeben

The way the public thinks about principals is derived from how they think about schools. The concept of schooling in most of the world is that it is a fundamental human right. The conventional wisdom suggests that schooling is responsible for preparing the nation's youth for future social, political, and economic success. Again, these are hard concepts to quantify, and frequently contradictory ones, as Barr and Dreeben suggest.

Throughout parts 1 and 2, a new way of thinking about principals was used to describe the growing American school principal crisis and to question the conventional wisdom that contributes to this crisis, respectively. In part 3, this new way of thinking about principals is openly defined, discussed, and used to redefine what school principals actually do and how the growing American school principal crisis can be averted.

The new way of thinking about schools is less focused on what individual gain youth and others immediately demonstrate and more focused on the collective aspects of schools as fiercely individual but also fiercely shared institutions. This means recognizing the permeability and adaptability of schools as well as the tendency to adhere to commonly held notions about what schools do—and for the overall tendency of schools and school systems to appear homogeneous in spite of tremendous differences.

With this shift in thinking about schools comes a shift in thinking about principals. If schools reflect commonly held notions about ways principals "should" be, then principals might not necessarily act rationally. The fact of the matter is that much of what principals do is not by rational decision-making, but rather because that is what is the norm, or "appropriate" for them to do.

In particular, this revives the question from part 2 about what school principals really do, and whether their characteristic activities and behaviors are more realistically defined as leadership or management. This is the question that only the few who seek to understand and to truly improve might ask, but it is an essential question to answer if a solution to the growing American school principal crisis is to be found. If American school principals really are becoming heavy-handed, what is it about their behavior and activity that sets them apart and contributes to this crisis? And perhaps more importantly, how can this crisis be solved?

CHAPTER 8

The New Institutionalism in Schools

New ways of thinking about schools and school principals require new approaches to familiar ideas. Since the late 1970s several new ways of thinking about organizations have arisen. As a result of the spread of public schools in every developed and most developing nations throughout the twentieth century, a commonly shared idea of what schooling is has become globally "institutionalized." Institutionalization means that there is a basic, internationally legitimate model for schooling that every educational system in the world conforms to regardless of differences in the cultural, political, social, or economic contexts that define individual school communities.

The institutionalized elements of schooling suggest that schools are generally public, professionally staffed, and "officially" undifferentiated within systems. Given these similarities in schools across national educational systems, is there also an institutionalized model for school principals' management activity that crosses national boundaries and transcends potentially unique elements of individual schools' environments?

The problem is that school contexts are unclear and cross traditionally understood organizational boundaries. This means that it is difficult to talk about where influences on schools and their principals begin and end. Are principals influenced by or accountable to their local community only or to state educational officials as well? Is the influence of the local environment stronger than the national-level stakeholders' needs and expectations for schools? It is often hard to answer these questions clearly because the influences at each level either mix with or are the result of the influences at the other.

This problem of broad and ambiguous definitions of schools' contextual boundaries is significant because "organizational environment" is a central concept of an institutional theory of organizations. An institutional approach to school principals is founded on the idea that schools are replete with rituals and loosely coupled relationships between what school principals do and what schools produce. Rituals and relationships in schools result from the influence of schools' cultural, political, social, and economic contexts. There is also attention to the public–private dichotomy in the management of organizations from this perspective. Because schools are public institutions, the contexts in which schooling occurs are significant, but the issues of environmental penetration are largely the same for both profit and nonprofit organizational sectors. It is largely a matter of degree.

First, consider the rituals inherent in schooling and school principals' roles. A ritual is any stereotypical or customary behavior or practice. What is it customary for principals to do as part of their official role in schools? Or what is stereotypical school principal behavior? Of course, the expectation that principals will ensure the smooth operation of their schools is important. But what school principals do has become largely ritualized. Take the hiring and evaluation of teachers as an example. The ideal and official concept is that principals hire based on qualifications and evaluate based on teachers' demonstrated instructional performance.

Now consider how this ideal, official concept is loosely coupled to the actual hiring and evaluation of teachers by principals. In reality, hiring decisions are often driven more by supply and demand than by an objective standard. For example, during a recent school visit I asked a school principal why she hired a certain teacher known to be of lesser quality. The immediate and matter-of-fact reply was "Because I needed a special education teacher, and she is certified." So, if a teacher is state-certified and a position is vacant, that is often enough justification for hiring that teacher.

The evaluation of teachers is similar. The ideal and official concept is that principals make several observations of a teacher and base their evaluations on objective criteria applied to those observations. Again, the reality is often quite different from the ideal. Many principals visit a teacher's classroom only once because of their own time restrictions or base their evaluations on whether any parents complained about that teacher. In both of these cases, the hiring and evaluation of teachers are rituals in a school principal's life. They are customary practices that have been imbued with more meaning and significance than the actual activities objectively merit.

As a frame for addressing the issues of ritual and coupling, Jane Hannaway (1989, pp. 3–5), director of education policy at the Urban Institute, suggests three themes for managerial activity that provide a framework for the activity of principals and the influence of schools' organizational environmental complexity on this activity. Hannaway's themes are (1) the usefulness or effectiveness of the activity, (2) the reliance of the activity on cues from the social structure of the system, and (3) the measuring of the results of the activity by others, which links it to others' perceptions rather than to the objective measurement of performance.

These three themes of managerial activity emphasize the results, responsiveness, and relativity of what school principals do and roughly align with the achievement, accountability, and access expectations discussed in part 2. In particular, the results refer to the "bottom line" for school principals. This usually means progress or gain in student achievement when educational policy and school principals are being discussed. The responsiveness theme for school principals relates to the contextualization of principals' behaviors and activities. School principals adjust their behavior within certain organizational limits to fit the specific needs and wants of the students, parents, and community of their particular school. Finally, the relativity theme emphasizes that there is variation in what goes on in schools and how school principals act from one school to the next. School principals' activity is relative to their school and community.

The responsiveness and relativity themes, in particular, suggest that there is a lot of juggling of legitimate behavior within and across the various school environments. What principals do does vary based on local needs and concerns, but the variation is limited by what is considered legitimate or appropriate for school principals to do in their particular educational and sociocultural system. There are times when what principals do disconnects from what is considered appropriate. These disconnects are usually not too extreme and are typically expected, but they do occur, and they embody the concept of "loose coupling."

Specifically incorporating the idea of school principals as managers rather than leaders into both the school administration and public discourse is dependent on the degree to which these discussions take place with an understanding that schools are global institutions and that the mass schooling model is fundamentally democratic. One of the limitations of identifying school principals as managers rather than leaders is that the stereotype of a manager is not one of a change agent but one of a bureaucratic functionary. Yet managers in institutionalized organizations like schools *are* agents of change. The difference between what school principals as managers are and what the popular expectations for school principals as "leaders" are is one of unit rather than effect. To dispel the stereotype of managers as bureaucratic functionaries, a discussion of various explanations for change in schools and schooling is helpful.

Change does occur through institutions like schools. Sociologist Ronald Jepperson (1991, p. 159) suggests that the "reification of action, rooted in the larger institutional matrix of American society, has promoted the taken-for-grantedness of action and has simultaneously hindered scholarly perception of institutional effects." An exploration of institutional change emphasizes the distinction between technical and institutional environments.

One of the clearest explanations of the distinction between the technical and institutional environments comes from two Stanford sociologists, W. Richard Scott and John W. Meyer (1991, p. 123). They say that *"technical environments* are those in which a product or service is produced and exchanged in a market such that organizations are rewarded for effective and efficient control of their production systems." This definition closely aligns with the instructional leadership approach discussed in chapter 5 and is remarkably similar to the achievement and accountability expectation environments for school principals emphasized in the conventional wisdom. In contrast, *"institutional environments* are . . . characterized by the elaboration of rules and requirements to which individual organizations must conform if they are to receive support and legitimacy."

Outcomes of organizations (such as school performance or student achievement) and individual participation in organizations (such as school principals' behavior and activity) are not necessarily as important in an institutional environment as they are in a technical one. This separation of process from outcome is fundamental to institutional approaches to change and reform that emphasize management over leadership. Institutional perspectives on schooling in their most extreme sense suggest the persistence of structures and processes without, necessarily, any accompanying outcomes.

Jepperson (1991, p. 153) further suggests that environmental contexts and collective agency are strong influences and can lead to action bringing change through contradictions or opposition to institutionalized social elements. Strong external influences can initiate change in schools' institutional structures and procedures. According to Jepperson, these "contradictions . . . can force institutional change by blocking the activation of reproductive procedures or by thwarting the successful completion of reproductive procedures, thus modifying or destroying the institution." Changes in institutions like schools that occur as a result of pressures from a school's environmental context suggest that agency is at work, but more so at the organizational level than at the individual level.

Change does not have to be initiated by severe elements outside of the institution. Although institutional forms and scripts may be applied very uniformly across many school environments, individuals and schools may "shop" for the schooling model they prefer depending on the context and situation in which they will apply it or conform to it. The interactive character of legitimacy-seeking is interesting given that outcomes of institutional structures and processes often do not change in spite of changes in form and script that may occur.

The main criticisms of institutional approaches to school principals' behavior and activity, especially ones emphasizing management over leadership, focus on questions of rational choice and decision-making. Without active participants, rational choice and decision-making cannot exist, and without the option or ability to rationally make decisions, some have suggested that institutional approaches do not allow for the humanity and reality of school change, growth, and even (organizational) death that can be observed in every situation, environment, and cultural context and in particular in the managerial activity of school principals.

What does this mean in relation to school principals and what they do? This new way of thinking suggests that schools as organizations are collectively bound together as an institution, and that because of their institutional character they are limited or directed as much by a legitimate schooling model as by local or immediate conditions. The behaviors and activities of school principals in each school system depend on the factors that determine the legitimacy of each national system or the type of legitimacy each school or school system seeks in their unique context.

THE MORE THINGS CHANGE, THE MORE THEY STAY THE SAME

American schools succeed and survive as a result of something called institutional isomorphism. Institutional isomorphism in schools is the gradual tendency for schools and schooling to become more similar or alike over time. This means that the structure, process, and content of schooling becomes more alike both within and between national systems of education. In so doing, the legitimate model for schooling shifts the emphasis away from the technical output or efficiency of schools. Instead, the achievement, accountability, and access expectations for schools reinforce schools' dedication to legitimate structure and certification both nationally and in an international context. Adherence to institutionally legitimate structure remains even within school systems where the activities of students, teachers, and even school principals decouple from that structure.

Variation in what school principals do from school to school, as well as from system to system, is a function of the complexity of both the institutional and technical environments of schools. What principals do is driven more by outside institutional pressures than by internal concerns for technical output. This is not to say that technical output like student achievement is not part of the environmental mix for schools or is not a concern of principals. A loosely coupled model suggests that many other objectives occupy principals' time and efforts, and these are often institutionalized requirements from outside of schools and school systems.

Is there an internationally institutionalized model for school principals' activity? Previous studies have determined how schools' organizational structures and curricula are institutionalized or shown that teachers follow institutionalized norms for behavior and activity that do not necessarily correspond to cultural or regional traditions (Meyer, Ramirez, & Soysal, 1992; LeTendre, Baker, Akiba, Goesling, & Wiseman, 2001).

There is evidence that there are norms for school curriculum and classroom instruction that transcend local or regional idiosyncrasies and are relatively standard in many otherwise dissimilar national systems of contemporary mass schooling (Benavot, Cha, Kamens, Meyer, & Wong 1991). In the broadest sense, schools are generally large-scale and organizationally complex due to high enrollment rates, long periods of formal schooling, and increased access and opportunity for a wider swath of potential students—all of which are results of the institutionalization of schooling as a mass, compulsory institution.

CHAPTER 9

The Complexity of School Principals' Work

There are no easy answers. Between the multiple expectations, multiple contexts, and multiple administrative systems within which schools and school principals operate, determining what American school principals either are or should be doing is difficult to say at the least.

Across the many kinds of schools and educational environments that exist, there are often consistently similar pressures on principals to behave in certain ways and perform certain duties. Principals find themselves either looking to legitimate models of school principal behavior or being taught to be school principals in formally accredited professional training programs that follow rigid scripts in the training of school principals in order to maintain legitimacy themselves. The mechanisms of institutional isomorphic change consist of coercive, mimetic, and normative influences (DiMaggio & Powell, 1983). When considering principals' management activities, one might expect that what school principals do would become increasingly standardized and stable over time due to pressures to conform to the accepted model. These influences may lead school principals to follow models of principals' activity.

Following established, rationalized models ensures the legitimacy of school principals' activity even though some activities may not always align with specific school environments. This means that the activities of principals are sometimes torn between the rationalized models of legitimate school structures, processes, and outcomes and the characteristics and needs of principals' local school environments.

Archetypal models for school principals' management activity persist in spite of wide variation in school output by nation and by schools.

The public permeability of schools is largely to blame for the complexity of school principals' work. Of course, some experts have argued that too much has been made of the difference between public (nonprofit) and private (for-profit) organizations. These are bold assertions, which may suggest that there are institutionalized models for managerial activity regardless of organizational sector and environmental influence. The implications of these assertions support an institutional approach to principals' management activity, but there are flaws in saying that institutionalized organizational models that apply across both public and private institutions extend to schools as well.

There is something unique about principals as managers of schools that distinguishes them from managers in other organizations, both public and private. Among the many kinds of schools and educational environments that exist, there are still pressures on principals to behave in similar ways and perform duties leading to similar outcomes. These pressures often begin as district or state accountability programs. Principals may manage schools as institutionalized public organizations as much as they represent schools as locally, contextually situated organizations or even themselves as individual, authoritative administrators.

An example of the environment of accountability in schools is found in the No Child Left Behind legislation. The accountability requirements that have arisen from this revision of the Elementary and Secondary Education Act in the United States exist at every level of schooling, from the school-building level to the national level. Accountability plans have to be established and approved at the state and national levels; penalties apply to some schools as a result of their performance on the annual assessments administered as part of the accountability plans; and annual yearly progress standards have been set to measure the progress and performance of each school, district, and state both individually and in comparison to other schools, districts, states, and eventually nations.

LEGITIMACY AND ACCOMMODATION

The significance of environmental contexts such as those characterized by these accountability plans is that legitimate school principal activities depend on the particular alignment of the globally institutionalized legitimate model with each school, educational system, and broader context. School principals' management activity should vary depending on the national characteristics of schools' organizational environments.

Variation in what school principals do is contextualized by specific school conditions and communities. Principals who respond to school contexts and accommodate community needs should be more influential than principals who follow a strictly standardized model, which limits their decision-making authority. These school-specific conditions are nested in the larger national context determined in part by internationally institutionalized models of legitimate principal behavior and in part by the penetration of school management hierarchies and systems by environmental conditions. One way to describe the institutional models of school principals' activity by school system is to determine where school decision-making is located within the system.

Figure 9 shows the location of school decision-making control by nation for thirty-nine countries. The countries with educational systems in which most of the decision-making control is at the local level are listed toward the top, with the United States having the most localized and locally controlled school system among the nations listed. Countries with educational systems in which most of the decision-making control is at the national level are listed toward the bottom, with Romania, France, and Cyprus having the most centralized and nationally controlled school systems among the nations listed.

The locus of decision-making control is important for school principals because in systems where most of the decisions are locally decided, school principals will share and be responsible for a large number of these decisions. In systems where most of the decisions are nationally decided, principals will not have as much influence on what is said and done.

Regardless of the relationship between principals' activity and schools' local environments, centralization of decision-making at the national level may determine principals' ability or opportunity to contextualize instruction within their schools. The same institutional influences that contribute to the training, education, and activity of principals within rationalized and legitimate models of school administration are products of the environment and of preexisting levels of school performance at least as much as they are causes of it.

Mostly	USA
Local-Level	Canada
Decision-Making	Portugal
	Netherlands
	Australia
	Sweden
	Czech Republic
	Spain
	Switzerland
	Hungary
	Denmark
	Belgium (French)
	Norway
	Scotland
	Kuwait
	England
	Iceland
	Japan
	Ireland
	Lithuania
	Colombia
	Russian Federation
	Germany
	Korea
	Singapore
	Iran
	Austria
	Thailand
	Belgium (Flemish)
	New Zealand
	Hong Kong
	Israel
	Latvia
	Slovenia
	Slovak Republic
	Greece
Mostly	Romania
Nation-Level	France
Decision-Making	Cyprus

Figure 9. *Locus of School Decision-Making Control (Astiz, Wiseman, & Baker, 2002).*

Principals' management of both material and personnel resources is not as influential as the environment or context, which preexists schooling processes and permeates most aspects of schooling that students receive. School principals' management activity is caught between local school environmental pressures and national environmental pressures. As figure 10 shows, principals respond to (1) pressures at the system level for legitimacy, and (2) pressures at the local level for accommodation. Principals typically respond to these discrepant pressures by loosely coupling their behavior to both system-level models and local-level needs.

While some of the activity of principals as school managers surely follows technical-rational, bureaucratic models, the more organizational and institutional elements of managerial activity are frequently agency-less "actions" performed in accordance with legitimate, scripted models of activity. Yet to deny that these models exist, and that principals behave in a manner appropriate to maintaining not only their individual legitimacy but also the legitimacy of their schools in both local and national contexts, would be to deny the influence of organizational environment. What drives much of principals' actions is their attention to and need for legitimacy at both the local and national levels. Yet what constitutes legitimate activity at the local level may not and often does not correspond to what constitutes legitimate activity at the

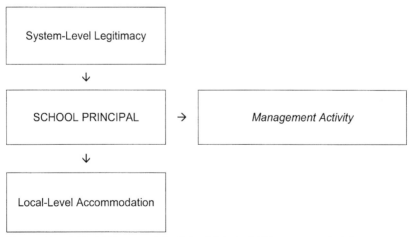

Figure 10.   *A Model Framework for School Principals' Management Activity.*

national level. While certain management activities and organizational outputs may be desired at both levels, the process or method of achieving these activities and outputs may vary significantly from system to system or from school to school.

ADMINISTRATIVE VS. INSTRUCTIONAL MANAGEMENT

It has so far been established that school "leadership" is a frequent misnomer, but what kinds of management activity do school principals engage in instead? The core types of principals' management activity are administrative and instructional management. Studies show that principals spend much of their time either performing administrative duties or supporting the teachers and others who have direct contact with students—usually contact involving instruction.

Administrative management encompasses the activities that principals do to maintain the basic organizational functions and structure of schools. This includes but is not limited to personnel and resource management. In particular, principals' administrative management activities may include training teachers, fostering professional development activities, deciding course offerings, establishing student grading policies, hiring teachers, assigning teachers to classes, talking with parents, counseling and disciplining students, responding to requests from district and state education officials, representing the school in the community and at official meetings, and any of several other internal administrative tasks.

Instructional management includes any activity that enhances or supports classroom instruction. These management activities range from the modeling of teaching to the support of collaborative relationships among school faculty. Principals' instructional management activity may include discussing educational objectives with teachers, initiating curriculum revision and planning, determining which textbooks are used, determining course content, and teaching (including preparation).

Although there are some activities in this list that could be defined as "instructional leadership," they are few and strongly contribute to school management. Most of the principal activities listed here fall into the administrative management category. If principals spend the most consistent amount of their time managing the administrative functions of schools, why are they often forced to think of themselves as something they are clearly not? This is where the school leadership advocates overstep their bounds. Making school principals be CEOs of instruction when they are needed as managers is inappropriate and actually sabotages student learning and achievement, the very things that school leadership advocates say concern them the most.

WHAT SCHOOL PRINCIPALS DO

Understanding what principals do forms the basis for making new policies and helping principals fulfill their roles and complete their responsibilities. The evidence suggests that principals are largely managers. The most obvious and important next step is to ask what a manager is. Rosemary Stewart (1996, p. 3101), a well-known scholar and expert on managerial activity, suggests that the two simplest definitions are: (1) managers are anyone responsible for the work of others, and (2) managers are those above a certain level in the hierarchy of supervision.

Even such basic and honest definitions may not be appropriate given that one characteristic managerial activity is to delegate responsibility and authority, and managerial activity becomes ambiguous as it is diffused throughout the hierarchy of organizational supervision. This ambiguity and diffusion arises because managers pass their responsibility and authority to others who perform many seemingly managerial tasks. This concept has lately come to be known as "distributed leadership." As principals delegate responsibility and authority, activities that may be characteristically managerial may not belong to or be performed by principals exclusively. Thus, the nature of managerial work causes a fundamental problem in identifying managerial activity.

A second important conceptual consideration is that different fields define managers and their activity differently (Noordegraaf & Stewart, 2000). The context of management varies considerably over time and among people in similar positions both within as well as across nations and organizations (Stewart, 1996). The obvious distinctions between the broader fields such as business, economics, sociology, political science, and education, for example, may be made, but even finer distinctions, definitions, and perceptions of managerial activity are possible.

For instance, even public administration and school administration experts have different conceptions of managerial activity.

A third and most important consideration for school principals in particular (as mentioned at the beginning of this chapter) is the conceptual distinction between public and private sector management and even the distinction within the public sector between the political and the social services spheres. Education and schooling contexts provide situations in which the activity of managers is semipublic. On the one hand is the frequent push by, for example, educational stakeholders, researchers, and practitioners for the corporate model of management in schools. Yet "as traditional public sector values—such as representativeness, equality before the law, justice—are forced to compete with modern managerial values—such as economy, efficiency, effectiveness—inevitable tensions arise" (Noordegraaf & Stewart, 2000, p. 436).

These tensions are what may give rise to a loose relationship (i.e., loose-coupling) or even a broken relationship (i.e., de-coupling) between the managerial activity of principals and school environments. These tensions also suggest how the environmental complexity of schools may influence school principals' management activity and encourage it to couple differently with the organizational environment at different organizational levels.

Thus the conceptual considerations when defining managerial activity, and school principals' management activity in particular, are dominated by (1) the ambiguity of what constitutes managers' work or activities, (2) the perception or relative context of both the managers and those observing or studying managerial activity, and (3) the semipublic and tension-producing characteristics, responsibilities, and pressures of principals as school managers. This ambiguity suggests the need for a discussion of what to look for in principals as school managers.

The empirical analysis of principals' managerial activities also deserves careful consideration. In particular, there are two elements to consider before conducting empirical analysis of managerial activity: (1) the replication and synthesis of other studies, and (2) managers as "creative copers" (Martinko & Gardner, 1990; Noordegraaf & Stewart, 2000). A problem with the empirical measurement of managerial activity is that, typically, subordinates of managers respond to questionnaires and surveys about what the manager does and why. Because the managers themselves are frequently not asked to describe their own activity and behavior, the possibility of misinterpretation and shortsightedness is real and distinct. The first consideration, which suggests that other studies should be examined to determine the ways in which managerial activity has been defined and empirically measured, is of particular importance. Colin P. Hales (1986) conducted a seminal review in which he critically asked what managers do. He argued that the various lists of managerial activities found in previous studies were discontinuous and even inconsistent.

Ironically, Hales synthesized these lists of managerial activities into several common strands. He suggested that managers' activities include acting as figureheads and leaders of organizational units; acting as liaisons through the formation and maintenance of contacts; monitoring, filtering, and disseminating information; allocating resources; handling disturbances and maintaining work flows; negotiating, innovating, and planning; and controlling and directing subordinates. These strands of managerial activity make up the internationally legitimate model for school principal behavior. This represents the institutionalization of what school principals do and is the result of years of coercive, mimetic, and normative forces influencing the role of school principals.

In spite of this neat list of categories forming the internationally legitimate model for school principals, school principals as managers are also "creative copers," meaning that their activity is often a fluid and unreasoned response to immediate needs or crises influenced by the school's context or environment. The unique context of school principals' managerial activities may be as relevant as or more relevant than principals' individual background characteristics or training. This means that within the broadly defined list of legitimate characteristics of principals there is no concrete definition of school principals' managerial activity to be had—only a fluid, flexible, contextually situated mesh of activities that may be "managerial" given the right circumstances.

CHAPTER 10

Why School Principals Do What They Do

Who cares what school principals really do? This is not as flippant a question as it initially appears. In a discussion of what is right and wrong with American school principals, the behaviors and activities of principals are the key components. Understanding what principals really do and why they do it is the best way to understand how they fit into the larger school system. The traditional way of thinking about school principals as "leaders" is not the best way of understanding them because, in spite of the conventional wisdom, their roles and responsibilities are not related to power relationships and authority structures as much as to the management and support of students, teachers, or other school functions, programs, and personnel.

New ways of thinking about principals are needed that avoid the rhetoric about leadership that clogs the principal training programs and professional development efforts of individual principals. These new ways of thinking also need to identify and explain what school principals really do rather than try to turn them into CEOs or something else that they are not.

Thinking about school principals as managers instead of leaders is hard to swallow at first. Already school principals are underpaid and overworked, and taking away the prestige associated with leadership is one more strike against them in many ways. In forming this new way of thinking about school principals, it has to be emphasized that the "school leadership" of conventional wisdom is a false hope in the sense that it builds expectations about principals that the nature of school organizations is fundamentally pitted against. No matter how well-intentioned or how experienced or how prestigious those who speak of school leadership are, it is still like trying to fit a square peg into a round hole. The square peg of conventional leadership wisdom is the expectation that principals influence student achievement and are accountable for it, and the round hole is the overwhelming access expectation not only in the United States but in every nation with a modern mass schooling system. This mismatch contributes largely to the American school principal crisis.

At the root of these square-peg expectations of achievement and accountability for school principals lies the misconception of principals as school leaders exclusively—and all of the baggage that the leadership moniker brings with it. The key failing of the conventional wisdom that school principals should be the power and authority players in the school organization is the fact that school principals are fundamentally managers. The nature of the job is management, and while there are elements of leadership that then enhance a school principal's management activities and behaviors, it is not the other way around. Management, not leadership, is the core characteristic of what a school principal really does.

Separating the expectations of school principals as leaders from the fact that their work is overwhelmingly managerial is difficult because the school administration system in the United States and similar systems in other nations have at various times attempted to reform their schools according to the corporate model. This corporate model, which emphasizes performance (i.e., student achievement) and accountability, relies on a strong leadership component founded on power and authority relationships to reach its goals. These corporate model goals are different from the organizational objectives of mass schooling, which coincide predominantly with the managerial elements of school principal behavior and activity.

Distinguishing the work of school principals that is characteristically leadership oriented from work that is management oriented is the first hurdle to establishing a new way of thinking about school principals, but as mentioned before, the nature of managerial work is slippery (Hannaway, 1989). Those who empirically approach management studies recognize the malleability of managerial activity even though less empirical and more policy-oriented studies do not. The business administration and management communities have long struggled with defining and measuring managerial activity in both for-profit and non-profit organizations.

Rosemary Stewart (1996) argues that defining managerial activity has long been a source of confusion. She describes the sources of confusion as "terminology" and other "complexities." Chapter 9 showed that managerial activity has been defined in many ways that vary significantly depending on the managerial context or the perspective of researchers and participants. For now the struggle is simpler. Are principals leaders? Are they managers? Or are they both?

In chapter 5, principals' activity was defined as dimensions of instructional leadership that include (1) developing mission and goals, (2) managing the educational production function, (3) promoting an academic learning climate, and (4) developing a supportive work environment (Murphy, 1990). In chapter 3, management was defined as skills that are "less specific to particular problems, and more restricted to specific organizations and industrial sectors; deal with a succession of tasks in one system, rather than a series of discrete tasks occurring in separate locations; [and] rest on a broad, diffuse knowledge base which includes extensive local knowledge" (Noordegraaf & Stewart, 2000, p. 434). Neither of these definitions is detailed enough to list specific activities that uniquely qualify as management or leadership, but they are a helpful start when considering the actual day-to-day activities and behaviors of principals. As such, each definition can be refined.

LEADERSHIP VS. MANAGEMENT, REVISITED

As popularly conceived, leadership is manifested in behaviors and activities that develop mission and goals, establish a climate and environment conducive to achieving the mission or goals, and befit the organizational figurehead. More directly, leadership behaviors and activities of principals would be things like (1) discussing educational objectives with teachers, (2) engaging in and directing professional development activities, (3) hiring and firing teachers and other personnel to create a team, (4) counseling and disciplining students to influence the attitude and activity of other people in the organization, (5) representing the school in the community or at official meetings, and in some cases (6) working and teaching in the classroom itself to serve as a live model for the mission and goals of the school as an organization (Martin, Mullis, Smith, Gonzalez, & Kelly, 1999).

Management consists primarily of activities that are "behind the scenes." This does not mean these activities do not play a prominent role in the life, development, and maintenance of the school organization, but it does mean that these activities and behaviors are often more routine and involve delegating responsibility as much as doing the activity or behavior itself. Stated plainly, management activities of school principals may coincide with any of the so-called "leadership" activities described above plus the following additions: (1) initiating curriculum revision and planning; (2) training teachers; (3) determining which textbooks are used; (4) determining course content; (5) deciding which courses are offered; (6) establishing student grading policies; (7) assigning teachers to classes; (8) talking with parents; (9) responding to requests from local, regional, or national education officials; and (10) internal administrative tasks such as enforcing regulations, managing the school budget, or establishing a timetable.

Why the overlap between leadership and management activities? Because the same activities and behaviors may be done with different objectives or for different reasons. Those that are considered more stereotypically "leadership" rather than "management" overtly emphasize the development of the mission or goals of the school organization. Those that are considered more stereotypically "management" rather than "leadership" may still contribute to or work toward this mission and these goals, but do so less overtly. This is a subtle, but important, difference.

A more concrete difference is that leadership activities and behaviors are often motivated or directed toward establishing, securing, or maintaining authority and power positions through the development of mission and goals. Those activities and behaviors more characteristic of management do not focus on positions of authority and power as much as on achieving the mission or goals themselves by any means necessary, even if that means delegating or sacrificing authority and power to accomplish the mission or goals.

A school or educational system that is inherently democratic due to its universal and often compulsory nature does not coincide with a school principal who is more autocratic or heavy-handed in nature. The popular conception and implementation of "school leadership" *does not* complement the democratic school system. The management style described above does.

The interactions between what principals do and schools' organizational environments as well as between different levels or layers of those environments largely influence the ways in which principals manage their schools. In the United States, school principals are subject to these interaction effects to a greater degree than principals in other nations' systems because of the degree of decision-making localization and the number of influential stakeholders that are not only allowed but encouraged to penetrate the school system.

The relationship between schools' organizational environments and principals' management activity is more strongly associated than principals' agency and school outcomes such as student achievement. Schools' organizational environments are replete with norms for principals' management activity and pressures from various stakeholders and constituents. These organizational norms and pressures inherent in schools' environments both influence how principals act and the kinds of principals managing at specific schools. For example, a principal who relies on the participation and encouragement of parents in improving students' academic achievement will probably not last very long in a working-class community where most parents are busy with shift work and are suspicious or distrustful of schools themselves.

This sort of parent-inclusive principal is quite appropriate for middle- and upper-class schools, where parents not only have work schedules flexible enough for them to participate in their children's schooling but where they also want to participate because they had relatively successful academic careers themselves and value academic achievement in their own children. School principals' management activity is, therefore, a response to school environmental norms and pressures. Plainly stated, principals manage instruction according to organizational norms established by environmental pressures.

What principals do is indeed related to the environments of schools, and this relationship is further complicated by association at two levels. The concept of loose coupling can be straightforwardly introduced into this discussion and tied into the organizational approach to school principals by providing the opportunity for principals' management activity to couple to either the local environment, the national environment, or both. This argument suggests that school principals' management activity responds to schools' environmental conditions rather than that principals adjust their managerial activity to effect certain outcomes. The expectation is that school principals' management activity associates with both local and national environments.

Principals' activities are loosely coupled with students' performance and perhaps even decoupled from individual student achievement. The often hypothesized and assumed causal relationship between school principals' management activity and student achievement is nonsignificant in both multilevel and international studies, in spite of the preponderance of studies and reports at the microlevel or based on anecdotal evidence in support of the popular "school leadership" approach.

A loosely coupled relationship between organizational environments and principals' activity exists at the school level, but at this level any causal relationship is either eliminated or reciprocal. This conception of loosely coupled relationships suggests a fragmented external environment. The incompatible expectations (achievement and accountability versus access) lead to "buffering, building gaps between, loosely coupling, or decoupling formal structures from actual work activities" (Orton & Weick, 1990, p. 207).

This focus on the loosely coupled structures and contexts between hierarchical levels leads to a discussion of the effects of the centralization of a nation's educational system. Central goals and objectives of educational systems are not unique to centralized systems. Neither are they synonymous with tightly coupled goals, processes, and outcomes. Still, the characteristics of national school systems limit or contextualize how school principals respond to school-level complexity in the organizational environment.

Ultimately, a view of school principals as managers has to look at management as providing direction and subtle leadership rather than as a reaction to, response to, or mediating element between conflicting organizational and environmental demands. School principals' management activity buffers or absorbs the disconnect between national schooling structure and policy and local schooling implementation and outcomes without exerting influence on one or the other.

The relationship between local school environmental complexity and principals' management activity is a positive one, meaning that as local school environments become more complex, principals spend more time managing their schools. Vice versa, as school environments become simpler, principals should need to spend less time engaged in managerial activity, so that it is the complexity of local school environments that influences school principals' management activity more than individual elements of the environment. The nested relationship of local school environments within national environments suggests that the national environment limits or bounds the effects of local school environmental complexity on school principals' management activity.

The national-level organizational environment has a limiting or bounding effect on the relationship between school principals' management activity and school level environmental complexity. What principals do is a response to pressures from multiple levels and sources, and these responses are nested within national contexts that limit and shape them in the first place. Theoretically, then, there is a relationship between the larger environments within which schools are embedded and the tasks on which organizational managers such as school principals spend their time.

The relationship or association of managerial activity to the organization as well as the organization's environment (or, in Hannaway's phrasing, "the social structure of the system") and the relationship of either to the organization's output is the focus of loose-coupling arguments. The difference in tightly coupled organizations like businesses and corporations is that there is significant overlap and responsiveness between (1) managerial activity; (2) organizational environment; (3) social, political, and economic environments; and (4) organizational output.

In loosely coupled organizations like schools, there is still some overlap between what managers do and the environments (organizational and social, political, and economic) in which they do it. Managerial activity is not necessarily coupled to organizational output, and organizational output may be coupled to the organizational and social, political, and economic environments in ways that are uniquely independent of the ways that managerial activity is coupled to those environments.

In characterizing loose coupling, organizations expert Karl Weick (1983, p. 44) argues that "coupled events are responsive, but . . . each event also preserves its own identity and some evidence of its physical or logical separateness." Schools embody the stereotypical characteristics of loosely coupled organizations such as (1) unclear, diverse, or ambiguous organizational means and goals; (2) low levels of organizational control; (3) low levels of managerial authority; (4) high levels of employee autonomy; and (5) low levels of coordination of employees' productive activities (Ingersoll, 1993). Schools are the very antithesis of school leadership concepts. Coupling can occur both within and between organizational levels.

This organizational impact of loose coupling can be seen by comparing the organizational characteristics of schools, which are typically loosely coupled organizations, with businesses or corporations, which are often more tightly coupled. The differences are striking. In businesses or corporations, organizational means and goals are often clear and unequivocal because profit is the only reason for the organization to exist. There may be other means and goals as well, but in businesses and corporations they are all secondary to the primary and overarching goal of profit.

Schools do not have the luxury of such clear and unequivocal missions and goals. Many educational reformers and critics would like schools to think of achievement the way that businesses think of profit, but that is impossible. Schools as organizations may include achievement as a goal, but not necessarily the predominant goal. This becomes clearer when the other oft-discussed school goal of learning is included, because using achievement as the only measure of learning is wildly inaccurate. It is an inaccurate measure of learning because it assumes that the only important learning is that which can be assessed quantitatively. This assumption excludes learning that may not be related to the traditional content areas offered in school, and it does not take into consideration learning that is more behavior oriented than performance or assessment oriented.

The situation of school principals in loosely coupled organizations like schools can be better understood through the seven characteristics of loosely coupled systems suggested by Karl Weick (1983). These seven characteristics are that (1) loose coupling allows the persistence of some parts of organizations because organizations then do not have to respond to every environmental change, (2) loose coupling provides a sensitive sensing mechanism for adjustment to local environmental influences, (3) loosely coupled systems are good for localized adaptation, (4) loosely coupled systems can change more and have more unique solutions than tightly coupled systems, (5) breakdowns in one part of a loosely coupled system are isolated and not allowed to spread to other parts of the organization, (6) loosely coupled systems allow more self-determination by the actors, and (7) loosely coupled systems are less expensive than tightly coupled systems because they do not coordinate people as much as tightly coupled systems.

These seven characteristics of loosely coupled systems may be abbreviated as persistence, adjustment, localization, change, isolation, self-determination, and expense. School principals cannot operate as "school leaders" in this type of organization because of the amount of extreme flexibility and variation at every level as a result of these characteristics of schools as loosely coupled organizations. For instance, the structure of schooling has become institutionalized across schools and school systems, but the unique context of each school requires adjustment in policy and mission.

Regarding the penetration of stakeholders and special interests into school principals' decision-making, again there is some international variation between school systems, but within individual countries variation is largely insignificant. So the persistence of some parts of schools as organizations, particularly instructional time and curricular decision-making in the examples given previously, is a characteristic of schools as loosely coupled organizations. This persistence affects what school principals as managers do because it means that structural models for school scheduling and governance remain fairly constant from school to school, thereby limiting the influence individual school principals have in those areas.

Within these persisting school structures school principals may adjust what they do and what their school does according to local environmental influences. School principals as managers can and do locally adapt their activity to the needs and concerns of the local social, political, and economic environments as well as individual students' and teachers' needs and situations. This is a behavior unique to school principals as managers because with this sort of localized adaptation, even within the institutionalized and relatively stable structures of schools, the mission and goals of the organization are going to split based on each student's and teacher's unique situation. School principals are able to allow and manage change at many levels and in multiple forms. This would be antithetical to the popularized version of "school leadership" that characterizes conventional reform efforts.

A distinct advantage to managing schools versus "leading" them is that breakdowns in one part of the school or school system are isolated because of the localized adaptation that has been allowed and encouraged. This type of isolation of problems means that other parts of school organizations are not necessarily affected by a breakdown in one part of the organization or system. An example of this is seen in the achievement rankings that are so popular with educational reformers.

If the instruction and learning that occurs in one classroom or school is poor, it does not automatically follow that instruction and learning in that school's other classrooms or in other schools in the system is going to be poor or negatively affected in any way. There is a mixing effect of localized adaptation and structural persistence that causes a conflict in the roles and responsibilities of school principals. This conflict is more plainly seen in the frequent disconnect between the national standards and policy and local-level implementation of schooling.

As school managers tailor their activity to the specific needs of schools' local environments and as managerial pressure from the national educational system increases (i.e., these predictors increase or combine), the complexity of the school managers' organizational environment should rise as well. The more complex that schools' organizational environments are within national educational systems, the more loosely coupled the managerial activity of principals should be to the school and national environments.

WHAT SCHOOL PRINCIPALS DO . . . AGAIN

Even at this stage of the discussion, specifying the elements of school principals' management activity requires a closer look at the individual elements of managerial activity: (1) manager, and (2) activity. Because principals are the specific focus of this book, they are clearly identified as managers within structurally and contextually similar organizations, specifically, schools. Although school managers may be categorically defined as any school personnel responsible for school functions and outputs and ranked above subordinates in the supervisory hierarchy of the school organization, it is useful to further identify more of the specific managerial characteristics of principals as school managers.

In relation to Stewart's two simple and least ambiguous definitions of managers explained above, this designation of principals as "school managers" fits. For instance, principals are responsible for the work of other people in that the instructional performance of teachers, the administrative performance of support staff, and the academic performance as well as appropriate activity of students are all part of principals' responsibilities, and principals may be held accountable for such.

Rosemary Stewart's second simple definition of managers also fits the description of principals in that their position in the schooling hierarchy is above the foreman level (i.e., ranked above teachers in classrooms) on the works side of schooling (i.e., academic instruction and learning) as well as above the first level of supervision in the offices (i.e., departmental or administrative heads). Yet principals as school managers do not occupy the highest level in the hierarchy in that they are below the levels of both responsibility and supervision afforded district- or regional-level superintendents, whose influence and accountability spans across many schools and accompanying school environments.

Principals are the highest school-level managers with the responsibilities and rights thereof. The managerial activity of principals is of foremost concern in educational policy and reform initiatives. Their activity is a much more complicated project because of the complexity of principals' work and the tension that arises from mixing both legitimacy and accommodation activities.

CHAPTER 11

The Mixed School Principal Model

International evidence can tell us a lot about American principals. It tells us not only that what American principals do is a product of legitimate models for principal behavior, but that this behavior is also constrained by each school's context. The international evidence tells us that American principals must act uniquely depending on the type of students, teachers, and community in and around their school. American principals must also act uniquely depending on the degree and depth of penetration by this context and by the public into the daily workings and overall structure of each school and school system, respectively.

If there is this much variation and uniqueness, then how can American principals be held accountable for the performance of their students and schools? On what common ground do principals stand that they can be compared between schools as well as across districts or states? If accountability is going to occur, either it must be based on a standardized and centrally administered system of education or it must be individually specific and uniquely evaluated for each principal. Americans have chosen a radically localized system of education. It is up to Americans to evaluate students, schools, and principals accordingly.

Capturing the characteristics of school principals in as many as forty nations sounds daunting, perhaps even impossible. There is, however, recent international data collected as part of a background questionnaire for school principals in most schools participating in the Trends in Mathematics and Science Study (TIMSS) conducted under the auspices of the International Association for the Evaluation of Educational

Achievement (IEA) and administered in the United States by the National Center for Educational Statistics.

This international data is invaluable as a tool to look at what principals do not only within educational systems but across them as well. Understanding why American school principals are in crisis and how they are becoming heavy-handed requires that they be examined both within the American school system and internationally to see larger trends.

An important distinction between school systems is the degree of centralization of decision-making authority. How much leeway are school principals given to make decisions that are locally contextualized, as opposed to having to abide by relatively inflexible mandates from the central administration? In a study I conducted with M. Fernanda Astiz and David P. Baker, we described the centralization of educational systems using data from these TIMSS school principal questionnaires (Astiz, Wiseman, & Baker, 2002). We divided the results of our investigation into degrees of centralization of decision-making. We found three categories of centralization: centralized, localized, and mixed. The mixed category causes the most trouble and is the fastest growing among nations because it is a combination of nation- or state-level policymaking authority and local-level implementation responsibility.

What does a mixture of decision-making authority mean for school principals? First, it means that there are going to be conflicting pressures on school principals to adjust their behavior and activity based on the needs and expectations of the policymakers versus those of the students, teachers, and local community. Second, it means that the organizational environment of schools where principals work becomes infinitely more complicated. The key difference between a mixed system and a more straightforward situation such as a mostly centralized or mostly localized system is that the rules constantly change in a mixed system. What principals are expected to do one day, month, or year can change rather quickly, so that the next day, month, or year the expectations are completely different.

If there are global trends in what school principals do (and there are), then what is it that sets American school principals apart? The number one distinguishing characteristic of American principals versus school principals in other nations is a result of the localized nature of the present American educational system. Approximately 15,000 autonomous school districts operate within the United States. In each of these autonomous school districts, clearly defined organizational heads, otherwise called school principals, run relatively autonomous schools. This is not the case in other countries. It is impossible to find another national education system as localized as the American educational system.

Even in nations that give decision-making or governance control to regions or local districts, the fiscal and curricular decisions are never as independent as they are in the United States. This has some very positive benefits for school principals in America. They can operate their schools basically as they see fit, which leads to large variations in the activities and behaviors of American school principals. But the disadvantages are many as well. Fiscal inequality among American school districts means that many schools simply do not have enough money to cover basic operating costs. Principals in other countries are usually able to cover their costs because financial support is more centrally or evenly administered.

Given this variation in schools within the United States, and the variation in what school principals do between countries, it is fairly plain to see that managing schools is largely a function of a school's or school system's context. So what sort of environment principals work in will largely determine what they do, how they do it, and what the results of their activity are.

School principals in other countries are usually not the administrative autocrats that American school principals are encouraged to be, either. By virtue of the way that American school organizations are structured, there is a clear delineation of authority within individual schools, and school principals are at the top. In other countries, the concept is one of "head teacher" rather than school principal. In these systems, the "principal" is simply a teacher with more experience or one who agrees to perform some administrative functions in addition to classroom instruction, but whose main responsibility is to a single classroom and the students in it.

School-related behaviors and activities are those involving (1) communication with students, parents, and education officials; (2) instructional leadership; (3) administrative duties; and (4) teaching (including preparation). This information comes from a report by the International Study Center at Boston College and uses data collected from school principals in as many as forty countries participating in the TIMSS

(Martin, Mullis, Gonzalez, Smith, & Kelly, 1999). While the International Study Center report uses a slightly different definition of instructional leadership than has been presented here, the international results show clear differences between what American school principals do and what school principals in other nations do.

At all three levels of schooling (elementary, middle, and high school), American school principals rank first or second in the world in total time spent communicating with students, parents, and education officials. They are in the top third or half in amount of time spent "doing" instructional leadership. In contrast, American school principals rank at or below the international average in amount of time spent conducting administrative duties. They rank nearly last in the world in amount of time spent teaching in the classroom.

These rankings say some interesting things about American principals. For one thing, American school principals value communication. This is not surprising given the nature of our school system in the United States: universal and compulsory. Communication between school principals and others is a result of the access entitlement that surrounds schools. Nations that American policymakers and school reformers often compare the United States with, such as Japan, spend much less time communicating with students, parents, and other education officials. This may be due in large part to the different school governance system that Japan has. Because the Japanese system is so centralized, there is not a need to communicate to the degree that the American school principals do. It may also have something to do with the stereotype of the American school principal as a dynamic school leader or manager, whereas Japanese school principals are not necessarily expected to become involved in the daily workings of the school since much of the instructional content and teaching methods are standardized and centralized at the national level.

The time that American school principals dedicate to instructional leadership activities (according to the International Study Center's definition) is above average at each school level. Japan's average amount of time spent by school principals on the identified instructional leadership activities is almost identical to the American principals' reported time. The reasons for this similarity are less clear and may have more to do with an error in the specification of "instructional leadership" than with any substantive similarity between what American and Japanese principals do. If there is not a specification error, then this similarity suggests that even though American and Japanese school principals operate within vastly different educational systems (localized and centralized, respectively), the local-level behaviors and activities of school principals related to instruction are relatively constant across systems. In a way, this makes good sense.

Communication levels would naturally be very different because localized governance affects the base of stakeholders and the school's (and school principal's) place within this structure, but instructional activity and the activity that contributes to instruction (as instructional leadership supporters claim) would be tied more to the achievement and accountability aspects of a school principal's job than to the legitimization of a school through direct communication with the stakeholders. From this perspective, being an instructional leader is a form of legitimization.

The amount of time that American school principals spend on administrative duties is virtually at the international mean. The administrative or managerial activities that all principals must engage in do not vary as much as the other activities. This is important. It is interesting to note that Japanese school principals spend much more time on administrative duties than do American principals. Again, the nature of their schools' organizational environment may be a significant determinant of the type of activities that school principals engage in and for how long.

It is amazing how little time school principals in the United States spend teaching in actual classrooms compared to the international average. American principals spend about twenty hours less per month teaching than do principals in other countries. For example, principals in Austria and the Netherlands spend more than sixty hours per month teaching while American school principals spend on average about five hours per month teaching. This figure is even more impressive in light of the fact that most American school principals are former teachers.

The upshot of all of this is again that tension that arises over legitimacy activities (defined as instructional leadership by the International Study Center in Boston) and accommodation activities measured by communication levels with students, parents, and education officials. This is the tension that produces the American school principal crisis.

CHAPTER 12

Averting the Crisis

What is the school principal's role in America's or any other country's system of education? Is it to be recognized? Is it to be prominent? Is it to stand alone for whatever it is each principal believes in? The best answer to these questions is no. The principal's job is to manage. To make sure that the school operates smoothly and meets the objectives of the organization, whatever they may be. We know that the large and long-term goals of most schools and school systems involve the education of students. But shorter-term and more immediate goals often simply address the function of the school. Does everyone have a place to park? Are parents able to communicate their needs and be listened to by school faculty and administration alike? This is the role of the school principal. Yes, instruction is a part of that, but "leadership" is not necessarily a part of the school principal's job description in the United States or in any nation.

The American educational system is organized in such a way that the public has control of and, ideally, responsibility for the schooling that occurs in their community. Unfortunately, in the growing popular "panic" of American educational reform, school principals are often pressured into becoming heavy-handed in this otherwise open and democratic system. While certainly an unfortunate choice, heavy-handedness is a common survival mechanism among cornered American school principals.

It is not easy to be heavy-handed in otherwise democratic school systems. For one thing, the heavy-handed school principal is remarkably alone and unsupported. When school principals eliminate shared responsibility even when it formally exists as part of the bureaucratic structure of schools, they often end up out on a limb all by themselves.

This only exacerbates the expectation and pressure that drove them to become heavy-handed in the first place.

The popular principal expectations of achievement, accountability, and access coupled with the assumptions that schools are like businesses, principals are like CEOs, and the myth of individual exceptionalism are nasty things for school principals to deal with. The idea of someone who is ultimately in charge and without the burdensome fetters of shared responsibility does seem to support the concept of "getting things done" and "the freedom to make things right." These trade-offs are not acceptable.

School systems are one of the only universally compulsory government-sponsored institutions in the world. Everyone has to go to school. This potentially makes schooling a very dangerous institution. The way to eliminate the totalitarian overtones of modern mass compulsory schooling is to put the governance and responsibility for schools into the hands of local communities, and ultimately individual school districts, buildings, and even classrooms. This balance of universal compulsion and democratic localism is what makes schools work, but it is also what causes school-related conflict.

The popular version of "school leadership" often emerges, particularly in times of crisis and adversity. The problem is that previous ideas about "school leadership" have been limited because school contexts often lack clear borders and cross traditional boundaries. Investigating the American case in a global context tells us a lot about American school principals. Institutions like schools change as they globally expand and adopt increasingly legitimate structures and processes. Principals' actions are determined according to organizational norms and in response to environmental pressures triggered by each school's particular context. This is somewhat anticlimactic because it suggests that school principals do what they are expected to do. Although charismatic and active school principals exist, the normal school principal is more managerial and measured.

The role of the heavy-handed school leader is a familiar one from popular movies and television shows such as *Dangerous Minds*, *The Principal*, *Lean on Me*, and *Boston Public*. Yet, in spite of the attention paid to principals and teachers "leading" in tough times, there is little understanding of which characteristic activities emerge in which contexts.

What school principals do is largely a function of what their school is expected to accomplish and the characteristics of the people or community that make up both the organization and its environment. Instead of measured responses to and recommendations for school principals, the conventional wisdom often reflects the "get tough" or "take charge" attitude. Does school leadership really require school principals to become so heavy-handed in an otherwise democratic educational system?

Although individual principals may adjust their behavior to fit the needs and concerns of local school communities, there are institutionalized characteristics of schooling systems that set the legitimate model for principals' activity within each school system. Principals' opportunities to contextualize their specific activities at the local school level are nested within and limited by the educational system's structure and policies at the national level as well.

By adopting policies and actively pursuing improvement in student achievement, school principals establish or maintain legitimacy within their district, state, or national school system and do so at very low cost in terms of resources either used or committed. By adapting standard models of schooling, school principals can help raise basic levels of educational attainment, establish largely undifferentiated curricula, and encourage higher levels of student achievement.

International evidence shows us that American principals act uniquely depending on the type of students, teachers, and community in and around their school. The heavy-handed approach makes for good movie ticket sales, but not necessarily for good school management. American principals must also act uniquely depending on the degree and depth of penetration by this context and by the public into the daily workings and overall structure of each school and school system in crisis, respectively.

If there is this much variation and uniqueness in what school principals do, then how can American principals be held accountable for the performance of their students and schools? On what common ground do principals stand that they can be compared between schools as well as across districts or states? An understanding of why and how school principals act either must be based on a standardized and centrally administered system of education or it must be individually specific and uniquely explained for each principal in each school. There are common characteristics of school principals' management that associate with certain characteristics of schools' environments. So exactly why and how principals behave may not be estimable, but the general conditions for and characteristics of principals managing schools are.

Heavy-handed "leadership" is slowly becoming the norm in the United States and around the world. As achievement envy, access entitlement, and the accountability "monkey" become increasingly stronger and ingrained in school cultures and contexts, this crisis in "leadership" continues to grow. But there is a way to slow and even stop this trend toward autocratic administration of schools. Even though the pressures and expectations that contribute to the heavy-handed leadership crisis are difficult to pinpoint (since they are multiple isomorphic trends), school principals still have the freedom to determine their own destiny—shocking as that may sound given the extensive discussions in previous chapters of the overwhelming power of context to determine what school principals do. Because principals can change the course of their destiny, and because those who contribute to the context and isomorphic forces shaping what principals do can affect how principals act as well, there are several principles for school management that can help to avert the crisis.

PRINCIPLES FOR PRINCIPALS

What can principals and others do to avert the growing crisis of heavy-handedness among school principals in America? This crisis is deceptive because it is slow in the making. It is silently creeping through American schools and will one day be the norm rather than an isolated event unless something is done. Averting the crisis is not as difficult as it may seem, however. By carefully considering a few principles, school principals can safeguard themselves and their schools from becoming victims of heavy-handedness.

Management experts have used the principles summarized in figure 11 for years in consultation with all sorts of organizations, including public schools (M. Droege, 2001). Although presented as statements in figure 11, these principles are posed as questions below. Principals should ask themselves these questions and answer them honestly. Parents, policymakers, and others should think of one school and one principal at that school when asking and answering these questions in order to limit the contextual variation that can occur between principals even in the same school district.

KNOWLEDGE (INDIVIDUAL PRINCIPAL)	
IDENTIFY EXPECTATIONS	Know the access and achievement expectations at the school, district, state, and national levels.
ACCOUNTABILITY CRITERIA	Know what the exact accountability criteria are (performance, gains, total or selected accessibility).
AUTHORITY AND CONSEQUENCES	Know who has the authority to exact consequences for both meeting and not meeting accountability criteria.

ACTION (MANAGEMENT TEAM)	
SHARE RESPONSIBILITY	Share responsibility and manage resources to meet accountability expectations.
PLAN FOR THE UNEXPECTED	Avoid heavy-handedness by planning for the unexpected with a management team.

Figure 11.   *Principles for Principals (adapted from M. Droege, 2001).*

First, what are the access and achievement expectations at the school, district, state, and national levels? Access entitlement and achievement envy are formidable pressures that every principal faces. At times these pressures can seem overwhelming. Continuous questioning, lobbying, and criticism by everyone from the students themselves up to the level of the highest policymakers and business representatives relentlessly bombard principals. Realistically outlining what sort of access the public, parents, community members, and school officials are entitled to can immediately divert some of that pressure.

One of the best ways to determine who has the right to immediate access and when is to review case studies of various school situations. Another useful tool is to simply keep a log for one day (or one week, if possible) of the various people trying to gain access to the principal through scheduled appointments, unscheduled meetings, referrals from other administrators and teachers, and phone calls. In this log, jot down a sentence or two summarizing what the person wanted, what the situation was, and nothing else. In other words, what was the fire that needed to be put out? What was the personal crisis that a student or parent was having that they thought needed the principal's attention? What was it that the teacher or administrator felt they could not handle without the principal's help or attention?

At the end of the day (or week) take five minutes to review the list and descriptions. Trends will begin to emerge. It may be that parents, or district administrators, or English teachers are accessing the principal in question predominantly. One of the most negative aspects of access entitlement is volume, so when trends in access are identified, principals can begin to "own" their time. They can plan ahead of time to meet with certain key parents, administrators, or teachers. This identification of access expectations, access trends, and the reasons or situations behind these access expectations and trends allows the principal to avert the chicken-with-its-head-cut-off response. When principals are bombarded with requests (or demands) for access from parents, administrators, or teachers, they already will know who needs immediate attention and who can wait until a regularly scheduled time to discuss or solve the situation at hand.

The other expectation that needs to be understood is the achievement expectation. What sort of performance is expected of the principal, the other school administrators, the teachers, the students, and the school as a whole? Are the performance expectations the same for everyone? Who is doing the "expecting"? Are some expectations unreasonable, inappropriate, or off the mark? Once it is identified who has expectations and what kind of performance they expect from whom, the principal can again keep a log for at least a week of the achievement expectations for that school and principal. During the same five minutes that the principal updates an access log, the who, what, and why regarding achievement expectations can also be jotted down. Was there a group of local business leaders at the school board meeting complaining that the local schools were not preparing students to be productive workers? Was there a parent who was dissatisfied with the performance of her son's English teacher or her son's performance on the SATs? Did the district superintendent call and give a report on the school's eighth-grade state assessment scores?

Second, given these expectations, what is the school principal held accountable for? Is accountability for principals geared toward high-level performance, gains in achievement, responsiveness to all stakeholders or only a select few? Perhaps the district superintendent is calling to talk about poor student performance on the eighth-grade state assessments, but says that the assessments are not important. Perhaps the district superintendent calls about the same thing, but instead yells at the principal for half an hour because students are not performing at the levels she thinks they should be. The principal should take a careful look at what the trends in accountability for access and achievement are. If measurable access and achievement levels are being written into district, state, or federal educational policy, then these are important accountability points. If the wording is less specific or is unrealistic—like the Clinton administration's educational policy statement in Goals 2000 that said by the year 2000 American students would rank first in the world in math and science achievement—then accountability is less strict.

Third, who has the authority to hold the principal accountable and what are the consequences of both meeting and not meeting those expectations? Of course, not all accountability expectations are written into formal policy, legislation, or law. A thoughtful evaluation of the various accountability expectations identified by looking at the trends in access and achievement expectations can help principals rank accountability expectations. Is federal or state financial support tied to certain access or achievement levels? Is the principal's own job dependent on a certain performance level? Are the teachers, students, parents, or community affected positively or negatively as a result of either meeting or not meeting identified access and accountability expectations?

Be realistic in answering these questions. Begin by determining the minimum amount of access and achievement that is needed in order to maintain the school's current level of funding, reputation, teacher quality, and student learning. Which access and achievement expectations must be met in order to maintain the status quo? This is the minimum. Then determine what is realistic for the principal to do above and beyond maintaining the status quo given time and resource restrictions of the normal human within the contexts of that particular public school.

By taking these first three steps, much of the pressure related to access, achievement, and accountability expectations can be alleviated. And alleviating this pressure will reduce or eliminate principals' need or desire to become heavy-handed. But up to this point all of these principles have focused on individual principals, and one of the ways to easily fall into the heavy-handed syndrome is to rely exclusively on the principal for all of a school's management decisions and responsibilities.

Fourth, how can the principal share responsibility and manage resources to meet accountability expectations? Educational management researchers can talk about "distributed leadership" until they are blue in the face, but the heavy-handed crisis will not be averted until the conventional concept of leadership is squelched. Why? Because the popular understanding of leadership is not one of sharing or managing. The visionary change-agent archetype pervades all of the school myths that serve as the inspiration and model for much of what principals learn about school administration in principal training programs, much of what they hear from their colleagues and at professional meetings, and much of what they read in the journals and trade magazines related to school administration. So this question is key to averting the crisis.

Sharing responsibility is fundamental to the principalship in democratic public schools. It is important to consider who should share responsibility. Will the hierarchy of authority be steep and narrow or flat and wide? Too many cooks can spoil the pot, as the saying goes. On the other hand, principals who act like dictators in a democracy are destined for failure. Determining who should share responsibility for the management of a school begins with a review of the access trends, achievement expectations, and accountability consequences.

A principal dealing with the problems of an urban school—including issues of poverty, racial tension, and poor student achievement—may want to consider who keeps trying to gain access to deal with these issues. Are parents crying out for a voice in the alleviation of racial tension in their children's school? Identify parents who could be good partners in solving this problem and bring them onto the school management team. Are there teachers who are trying every trick in the book to interest and engage their students but constantly seek the principal's advice or permission to try new things? If so, some of these teachers may be the kind of partners that would productively contribute to a school management team.

Fifth, how can the principal plan for the unexpected with a management team? This final principle incorporates the wisdom of the previous four and becomes the most important barrier against heavy-handedness. Where there is a management team, there is no room for heavy-handedness. In fact, a management team that has been carefully and thoughtfully assembled by a principal will not only eliminate the need for heavy-handedness in response to achievement, access, and accountability expectations, but will also easily identify and confront heavy-handedness in the principal if it creeps in unawares.

Brainstorming the worst-case scenarios related to access, achievement, and accountability can help avert the crisis of heavy-handedness. Being prepared takes some time and commitment. It may take an extra Saturday every month. It may mean making concessions in one area in order to be prepared for problems that may arise without warning. But when the management team has taken the time to prepare, and has even gone through the steps and responsibilities of each management team member given a particular scenario, then when the unexpected happens there will be no surprise, no fumbling, and limited negative consequences for the school, principal, teachers, students, and all of the other stakeholders in the educational system connected to that school.

KEEP AWAY FROM COOKIE CUTTERS

These principles for principals are purposefully general. The minute that principals encounter prescriptions or supposed models for "good," "effective," or "successful" leadership, there is a problem. Context dictates everything a principal does, and what may be the perfect action for one principal in one situation may not be and rarely is the perfect action for another principal. There is no one definition of "good," "effective," or "successful" because every school has a completely different context, stakeholders, students, teachers, and principal. Even if success is defined as student learning, the possible variations of this definition are staggering: Is it average achievement level? Achievement gain? Curriculum covered? Learning applied to real-life situations?

There is no one right answer. In fact, all of these and more are the right answer in any of several given situations.

Principals as managers can diffuse the growing accountability policies for schools. Principals as managers maintain perspective on the degree of their own importance and power. Principals as managers cannot become heavy-handed demagogues. Instead, principals as managers have the flexibility and opportunity to respond to schools' unique contexts. Principals as managers can decide which managerial activities are appropriate given the unique context of schools and educational systems within which they operate. Principals as managers decide which activities are the most effective uses of their time and effort. Principals as managers keep their schools in perspective by constructively benchmarking their activity in their schools, regions, or districts against the expectations and consequences of that activity in their national and international communities as a whole. The school principals who manage first and lead second are the only principals who know where the buck stops and are ready for it to stop there.

References

Astiz, M. F., Wiseman, A. W., & Baker, D. P. (2002). Slouching towards decentralization: Consequences of globalization for curricular control in national education systems. *Comparative Education Review*, 46 (1), 66–88.

Baker, D. P. (1993). "Compared to Japan, the U.S. is a low achiever . . . really: New evidence and commentary on Westbury." *Educational Researcher*, 22 (3), 18–20.

Barr, R., & Dreeben, R. (1983). *How Schools Work.* Chicago: University of Chicago Press.

Benavot, A., Cha, Y., Kamens, D. K., Meyer, J. W., & Wong, S. (1991). Knowledge for the masses: World models and national curricula, 1920–1986. *American Sociological Review*, 56 (1), 85–100.

Berliner, D. C., & Biddle, B. J. (1995). *The manufactured crisis: Myths, fraud, and the attack on America's public schools.* Cambridge, MA: Perseus.

Blau, P. M. (1971). *The structure of organizations.* New York: Basic.

Blau, P. M., & Scott, W. R. (1962). *Formal organizations: A comparative approach.* San Francisco: Chandler.

Boyd, W. L. (1994). Rational choice theory and the politics of education: Promise and limitations. *Journal of Education Policy*, 9, pp. 127–45.

Bracey, G. W. (1998, September). Tinkering with TIMSS. *Phi Delta Kappan*, pp. 32–36.

Buchen, I. H. (2000, May 31). The myth of school leadership. *Education Week*, 19 (38), 35–36.

Colomy, P. (1998). "Neofunctionalism and neoinstitutionalism: Human agency and interest in institutional change." *Sociological Forum*, 13 (2), 265–300.

Copland, M. A. (2004). Leadership of inquiry: Building and sustaining capacity for school improvement. *Educational Evaluation and Policy Analysis* (Special Issue on Educational Leadership), 22 (4), 375–396.

Crossley, M. (1999). Reconceptualising comparative and international education. *Compare*, 29 (3), 249–267.

DiMaggio, P. J., & Powell, W. W. (1983). The iron cage revisited: Institutional
isomorphism and collective rationality in organizational fields. *American
Sociological Review*, 48 (2), 147–160.

Droege, K. L. (2004, April). Turning accountability on its head: Supporting inspired teaching in today's classrooms. *Phi Delta Kappan*, pp. 610–612.

Droege, M. F. (2001, November). The eight magic questions. Presentation at
the University of Tulsa, OK.

Duffy, F. M. (1996). *A practical uide to designing high performance schools.*
Delray Beach, FL: St. Lucie.

Duffy, F. M. (1997). Should educational supervision be influenced by business
management practices? Yes. In J. Glanz & R. F. Neville (Eds.), *Educational
supervision: Perspectives, issues, and controversies* (pp. 202–209). Nor-
wood, MA: Christopher-Gordon.

Firestone, W. (1985). The study of loose coupling: Problems, progress, and
prospects. In A. Kerckhoff (Ed.), *Research in the Sociology of Education
and Socialization, Volume 5* (pp. 3–30). Greenwich, CT: JAI.

Fletcher, T. V., & Sabers, D. L. (1995). Interaction effects in cross-national
studies of achievement. *Comparative Education Review*, 39 (4), 455–467.

Fuller, B., & Rubinson, R. (1992). Does the state expand schooling? Review
of the evidence. In B. Fuller & R. Rubinson (Eds.), *The political construction of education: The state, school expansion, and economic change* (pp.
1–30). New York: Praeger.

Gamoran, A., & Dreeben, R. (1986). Coupling and control in educational organizations. *Administrative Science Quarterly*, 31, pp. 612–632.

Grey, C. (1999). "We are all managers now"; "we always were": On the development and demise of management. *Journal of Management Studies*, 36
(5), 561–585.

Gronn, P. (2000). Distributed properties: A new architecture for leadership.
Educational Management and Administration, 28 (3), 317–338.

Hales, C. P. (1986). What do managers do? A critical review of the evidence.
Journal of Management Studies, 23 (1), 88–115.

Hallinger, P., & Heck, R. H. (1996). Reassessing the principal's role in school
effectiveness: A review of empirical research, 1980–1995. *Educational Administration Quarterly* 32 (1), 5–44.

Hannaway, J. (1989). *Managers managing: The workings of an administrative
system.* New York: Oxford University Press.

Haws, L. (2004). From the principal files: The principal shortage—why
doesn't anybody want the job? *Education World Online*, http://www.educa-
tionworld.com/a_admin/admin/admin197.shtml.

Heck, R. H., Larsen, T. J., & Marcoulides, G. A. (1990). Educational leadership and school achievement: Validation of a causal model." *Educational Administration Quarterly*, 26 (2), 94–125.

Hoffman, D. M. (1999). Culture and comparative education: Toward decentering and recentering the discourse. *Comparative Education Review*, 43 (4), 464–488.

Ingersoll, R. (1993). Loosely coupled organizations revisited. *Research in the Sociology of Organizations*, 11, pp. 81–112.

Inkeles, A. (1974). The school as a context for modernization (pp. 7–23). In A. Inkeles & D. B. Holsinger (Eds.), *Education and Individual Modernity in Developing Countries* (pp. 7–23). Leiden, Netherlands: Brill.

Inkeles, A. (1979). National differences in scholastic performance. *Comparative Education Review*, 23 (3), 391.

Jepperson, R. L. (1991). Institutions, institutional effects, and institutionalism. in W. W. Powell & P. J. DiMaggio (Eds.), *The new institutionalism in organizational analysis* (pp. 143–163). Chicago: University of Chicago Press.

Keller, B. (1998, May 20). In age of accountability, principals feel the heat. *Education Week*, pp.1, 16. Available online at http://www.edweek.org/ew/vol-17/36press.h17. Accessed April 12, 2000.

Kuroda, K. (1995). Effective school research from a Japanese perspective. Paper presented at the North-East/Mid-West Regional Conference of the Comparative and International Education Society, Buffalo, NY.

Lau, A. W., Pavett, C. M., & Newman, A. R. (1980, August). The nature of managerial work: A comparison of public and private sector jobs. In R. C. Huseman (Ed.), *Academy of management proceedings '80* (pp. 330–344). Fortieth Annual Meeting of the Academy of Management, Detroit.

Leithwood, K. A., & Duke, D. L. (1999). A century's quest to understand school leadership. In J. Murphy & K. S. Louis (Eds.), *Handbook of research on educational administration* (2nd ed.) (pp. 45–72). San Francisco: Jossey-Bass.

Leithwood, K. A., Jantzi, D., & Steinbach, R. (1999). *Changing leadership for changing times*. Buckingham, UK: Open University Press.

LeTendre, G. K., Baker, D. P., Akiba, M., Goesling, B., & Wiseman, A. W. (2001). Teachers' work: Institutional isomorphism and cultural variation in the U.S., Germany and Japan. *Educational Researcher*, 30 (6), 3–13.

Martin, M. O., Mullis, I. V. S., Gonzalez, E. J., Smith, T. A., & Kelly, D. L. (1999). *School contexts for learning and instruction*. Chestnut Hill, MA: TIMSS International Study Center, Boston College, International Association for the Evaluation of Educational Achievement.

Martinko, M. J., & Gardner, W. L. (1990). Structured observation of managerial work: A replication and synthesis. *Journal of Management Studies*, 27 (3), 329–357.

Meyer, J. W., & Baker, D. P. (1996). Forming American educational policy with international data: Lessons from the sociology of education. *Sociology of Education*, Extra Issue, pp. 123–130.

Meyer, J. W., & Rowan, B. (1977). Institutionalized organizations: Formal structure as myth and ceremony. *American Journal of Sociology*, 83 (2), 340–363.

Meyer, J. W., & Scott, W. R. (1983). *Organizational environments: Ritual and rationality*. Beverly Hills, CA: Sage.

Meyer, J. W., Ramirez, F. O., & Soysal, Y. N. (1992). World expansion of mass education, 1870–1980. *Sociology of Education*, 65 (2), 128–149.

Meyer, J. W., Ramirez, F. O., Rubinson, R., & Boli-Bennett, J. (1977). The world educational revolution, 1950–1970. *Sociology of Education*, 50 (4), 242–258.

Meyer, M. W. and Associates (Eds.). (1978). *Environments and organizations*. San Francisco: Jossey-Bass.

Mintzberg, H. (1980). *The nature of managerial work*. New York: Harper & Row.

Murphy, J. (1990). Principal educational leadership. In P. W. Thurston & L. S. Otto (Eds.), *Advances in educational administration: Changing perspectives on the school, Volume 1* (pp. 163–200). Greenwich, CT: JAI.

Noordegraaf, M., & Stewart, R. (2000). Managerial behaviour research in private and public sectors: Distinctiveness, disputes and directions. *Journal of Management Studies*, 37 (3), 427–443.

Ogawa, R. T., & Bossert, S. T. (1995). Leadership as an organizational quality. *Educational Administration Quarterly*, 31 (2), 224–243.

Orton, J. D., & Weick, K. E. (1990). Loosely coupled systems: A reconceptualization. *Academy of Management Review*, 15 (2), 203–223.

Ouchi, W. G. (1978). Coupled versus uncoupled control in organizational hierarchies. In M. W. Meyer and Associates (Eds.), *Environments and organizations*. San Francisco: Jossey-Bass.

Paige, R. M., & Mestenhauser, J. A. (1999). Internationalizing educational dministration. *Educational Administration Quarterly*, 35 (4), 500–517.

Ramirez, F. O., & Meyer, J. W. (1980). Comparative education: The social construction of the modern world system. *Annual Review of Sociology*, 6, pp. 369–399.

Ravitch, D. (2000). *Left back: A century of battles over school reform*. New York: Simon & Schuster.

Reynolds, C. (Ed.). (2002). *Women and school leadership: International perspectives*. Albany, NY: State University of New York Press.

Rose, L. C., & Gallup, A. M. (2003). The 35th annual Phi Delta Kappa/Gallup poll of the public's attitudes toward the public schools. Accessed August 25, 2003 at http://www.pdkintl.org/kappan/k0309pol.pdf.

SCANS (Secretary's Commission on Achieving Necessary Skills). (1991). *What work requires of schools: A SCANS report for America 2000.* Washington, DC: U.S. Department of Labor.

Schmidt, W. H., McKnight, C. C., & Raizen, S. A. (1997). *A splintered vision: An investigation of U.S. science and mathematics education.* Boston: Kluwer.

Scott, W. R., & Meyer, J. W. (1991). The Organization of societal sectors: Propositions and early evidence. In W. W. Powell & P. J. DiMaggio (Eds.), *The new institutionalism in organizational analysis* (pp. 108–140). Chicago: University of Chicago Press.

Sergiovanni, T. (1996). *Leadership for the schoolhouse.* San Francisco: Jossey-Bass.

Simon, H. A. (1976). *Administrative behavior: A study of decision-making processes in administrative organizations.* New York: Free Press.

Spillane, J. P., Halverson, R., & Diamond, J. B. (2001). Investigating school leadership practice: A distributed perspective. *Educational Researcher*, 30 (3), 23–28.

Stewart, R. (1976). *Contrasts in management, a study of different types of managers' jobs: Their demands and choices.* London: McGraw-Hill.

Stewart, R. (1982). *Choices for the manager.* Englewood Cliffs, NJ: Prentice Hall.

Stewart, R. (1996). "Managerial behaviour." In *International Encyclopaedia of Business and Management*, M. Warner (Ed.). London: Thomson Business Press, 3100–3116.

Tozer, S. E., Violas, P. C., & Senese, G. (2002). *School and society: Historical and contemporary perspectives.* Boston: McGraw-Hill.

Tyack, D. B. (1974). *The one best system: A history of American urban education.* Cambridge, MA: Harvard University Press.

U.S. Department of Education. (2002). *The use of scientifically based research in education: A working group conference, February 6.* Washington, DC: Author.

U.S. National Commission on Excellence in Education. (1983). *A nation at risk: The imperative for educational reform.* Washington, DC: U.S. Government Printing Office.

Weick, K. (1976). Educational organizations as loosely coupled systems. *Administrative Science Quarterly*, 21 (1), 1–21.

Weick, K. (1983). Educational organizations as loosely coupled systems. In W. Foster (Ed.), *Loose coupling revisited: A critical view of Weick's contribution to educational administration* (pp. 42–63). Victoria, Australia: Deakin University Press.

Weick, K. E., & Westley, F. (1996). Organizational learning: Affirming an oxymoron. In S. R. Clegg, C. Hardy, & W. R. Nord (Eds.), *Handbook of organization studies*. London: Sage.

Westbury, I. (1992). Comparing American and Japanese achievement: Is the United States really a low achiever. *Educational Researcher*, 21 (5), 18–24.

Westbury, I. (1993). American and Japanese achievement . . . again: A response to Baker. *Educational Researcher*, 22 (3), 18–20.

Winerip, M. (2003, August 13). The "zero dropout" miracle: Alas! alack! a Texas tall tale. *New York Times* (late edition—final), p. B7, col. 1.

Wiseman, A. W., & Goesling, B. (2000, April 25). Curricular centralization, principals' behaviors, and student achievement: A cross-national examination of cause, coincidence, and consequence. Paper presented at the American Educational Research Association annual meeting, New Orleans.

Index

About the Author

Alexander W. Wiseman is currently assistant professor of education in the School of Education at the University of Tulsa. He has taught at Aztec High School in New Mexico and in Kameoka, Japan, with the Japan Exchange and Teaching (JET) Programme. He received his B.A. in letters from the University of Oklahoma, his M.A. in international comparative education from Stanford University, and a dual-degree Ph.D. in both educational theory and policy and comparative and international education from Penn State University. He writes, teaches, and presents regularly on the managerial activity of principals, the school-to-work transition, and internationally comparative analyses of national educational systems. His publications include several books and numerous peer-reviewed articles in journals such as *Educational Researcher*, *Educational Evaluation and Policy Analysis*, *Public Administration and Management*, *Comparative Education Review*, and *Compare*. He lives with his family in Tulsa, Oklahoma.